ANDY IRVINE – AN AUTOBIOGRAPHY

An Autobiography

Andy Irvine

with Ian Robertson

Stanley Paul
London Melbourne Sydney Auckland Johannesburg

To Audrey, the children and my mother
for all the help and support over the years
when I've been away for days, weekends, weeks and even
months playing rugby

Stanley Paul & Co. Ltd
An imprint of Century-Hutchinson Ltd
17–21 Conway Street, London W1P 6JD

Hutchinson Publishing Group (Australia) Pty Ltd
PO Box 496, Hawthorn, Melbourne, Victoria 3122

Hutchinson Group (NZ) Ltd
PO Box 40–086, Glenfield 10, Auckland

Hutchinson Group (SA) Pty Ltd
PO Box 337, Bergvlei, 2012 South Africa

First published 1985

Set in Baskerville by Tradespools Ltd, Frome, Somerset

Printed and bound in Great Britain by
Anchor Brendon Ltd, Tiptree, Essex

British Library Cataloguing in Publication Data
Irvine, Andy
    Playing back: my life in Scottish rugby.
    1. Irvine, Andy   2. Rugby football players—
    Scotland—Biography
    I. Title   II. Robertson, Ian, *1945*—
    796.33'3'0924   GV944.9.17

ISBN 0 09 162270 0

Contents

Acknowledgements

I would like to thank Ian Robertson, the BBC rugby correspondent, for all his help in the preparation of this book, and especially for making so many trips to Edinburgh. I have told my story entirely in my own words, but the end product is the result of some careful and patient editing. After countless hours of relaying my thoughts into a tape recorder, Ian has structured and pruned nearly 400,000 words into the final script. I am particularly pleased that the book reflects so exactly my own thoughts and feelings.

I should also like to thank the secretarial pool which was headed by Mandy Easterbrook. I am very grateful for her tremendous dedication and speed, and also to Linda Gorrie, Ann Davies, Julia Robinson and Barbara Moller for their help.

I am also greatly indebted to Colin Elsey of Colorsport for providing so many excellent action photographs and for even managing to find a few which do not feature my tongue sticking out.

I would like to thank the Scottish Rugby Union for their cooperation in accepting my share of the proceeds from this book and passing the money on to charities of my choice.

Finally, I would like to thank my very understanding wife, Audrey, for all her help and encouragement, and also my publisher Roddy Bloomfield for his advice, guidance and patience.

1

Looking Back

George Orwell, in his most celebrated book, prophesied that 1984 would be a very special year. He was right, though I have to confess it is just conceivable that Scotland winning the Triple Crown for the first time since 1938 and the Grand Slam for the first time since 1925 were not the watersheds in the evolution of civilization he had in mind as he put pen to paper all those years ago.

However, for every man, woman and child born and living north of the border, where sporting success in global terms is rather ephemeral, 1984 will burn brightly in the memory for many years to come even if my own particular joy as Scotland left the field victorious over the French at Murrayfield was tinged with the inevitable hint of disappointment that when the final whistle blew I was not actually on the field to experience the full impact of Scottish rugby's greatest moment for 59 years.

In the past 20 years Scotland have produced a few individual champions like Grand Prix drivers Jim Clark and Jackie Stewart, boxers Ken Buchanan, Jim Watt and Walter McGowan, athlete Alan Wells and jockey Willie Carson, but in team sports only Celtic had proved supreme in winning the European Cup in 1967. Scotland's soccer squad have reached all the World Cup finals in recent years but, once there, their progress has been uninspiring and has lacked distinction. It was no surprise then that the entire nation of 5 million people were united in a common bond as the impossible dream became euphoric reality. For the first time in 11 years of international rugby I was a replacement sitting in a tracksuit for the two crucial matches against Ireland and France. I sat in the stands at Lansdowne Road and Murrayfield for both those epic encounters and I can honestly say that I relished each moment of triumph to the full, though I suppose the taste of victory would have been even more memorable if I had been in the team.

After all, I had played 51 internationals out of 52 between 1972 and 1982, and from the very moment I put on a Scottish jersey for the first time my great ambition had been to be part of a Triple Crown winning side. As I sat in Dublin watching Scotland destroy Ireland and romp away to a thoroughly convincing and impressive victory I was able to cast my mind back over a dozen unforgettable years with Scotland and take some consolation from the fact that all the good sides I had played in with so many great players and characters had, to some extent, perhaps played a small part in laying the foundations of the ultimate triumphs.

From playing against New Zealand in December 1972 to my last game for Scotland against Australia in Sydney in 1982, I was extremely fortunate that I missed only one match despite the fact that latterly I had to carry a few injuries. In consequence, it would be churlish to bemoan too strongly the run of wretched luck which plagued my career in the two years which followed that Australian tour until I announced my retirement from international rugby after the Grand Slam triumph.

My problems began when I injured a knee in a seven-a-side tournament in Edinburgh in April 1979 and I was unable to run properly for two months. By July, I reckoned it was time to start training for the new season, so I went out for a five mile run round the streets of Edinburgh. The next morning my calf muscles and my Achilles tendons were extremely stiff and sore. After a couple of days, the calves had eased off but the Achilles tendon never fully recovered, and I have been troubled intermittently ever since. I tried to play right through the opening two months of the new season because I was captain of Heriot's, and I was desperately keen to play in all the early league matches as we set out to retain the league championship. I endured eight weeks of unmitigated agony. Visits to doctors, specialists and physiotherapists failed to produce a cure, although I enjoyed spells when the pain was relatively bearable. During the next few years I was always conscious of the nagging, niggling pain of Achilles injuries which fellow sufferers will know only too well, and other people will probably never fully comprehend. The tendons were often so tender and sore first thing in the morning that walking unaided to the bathroom was a major and painful undertaking. The condition meant that despite the fact that I have always loved training, I was never again able to train as hard as I would have wanted.

Some days were very much better than others, and I did usually manage a rest between the end of one season, a summer tour and the start of the next season. Curiously enough, I suffered surprisingly little reaction during the tour to Australia in the summer of 1982 on the hard grounds out there, and I played my best rugby for a long time.

This rekindled my enthusiasm, and after a month's rest I began training in early August for the start of the next season. At the end of a sharp, hard training session I pulled a hamstring in a sprint. Then, when I resumed training, my Achilles tendon started to play up badly, causing considerable pain. I missed Scotland's match against Fiji, but after playing most Saturdays I was picked for the opening international against Ireland in January. Unfortunately, it took me five or six days to recover from a Saturday match before I could run properly again which totally precluded the possibility of running in training. From one Saturday to the next, I was unable to do much worthwhile training in between. After playing on the Saturday before the Irish game I had to tell the selectors that I would not be able to run around at their special squad session on the Sunday or even the next Thursday, two days prior to the match but

11

I would probably be able to play at Murrayfield against Ireland on the Saturday. In the circumstances, they were fully entitled to ask me to stand down. The pain had been so persistent and so intense that I had missed all three Scotland squad sessions between August and January and, quite naturally, I had lost not only some credibility with the selectors and the other players but a couple of yards of pace which were vital to my style of play. The situation had become absurd, and eventually the honorary surgeon to the SRU, Donald McLeod, and the team physiotherapist, David McLean, who had jointly spent countless hours treating my injury, felt that surgery would be the only satisfactory solution. I was very grateful to them for all their help and advice. I underwent an operation on my right Achilles tendon three weeks later in February 1983. This was very kindly arranged for me by the Scottish Rugby Union, and I would like to pay tribute to the surgeon at the Princess Margaret Rose Hospital in Edinburgh, Mr Michael McMaster, who did such an excellent job. The right leg had always been much the more troublesome, and the operation was a tremendous success. I had to rest for the next four months, and that enforced lay-off was exactly the break I needed to cure the trouble with the left Achilles tendon.

When the Grand Slam season began I was revitalized, free from injury and pain for the first time in four years, and I was determined to try to regain my place in the Scotland side.

I trained hard in August, and played the first six games of the new season in September for my club, Heriot's, recapturing some of my old form. We were undefeated, and the prospect of a final season in international rugby was not out of the realms of the possible. Then I pulled a thigh muscle badly in a club game and was out of action for the whole of October and November. I struggled back to fitness in December, but no sooner had I started playing again than I injured my acromio-clavicular joint which ruled me out for the rest of December and the whole of January. By the time I resumed playing, Scotland were already two-thirds of the way to the Triple Crown and half-way to a Grand Slam with wins over Wales and England. To my surprise and delight, having played hardly any rugby at all since the end of September I found that, after surviving just one comeback match in February for Heriot's, I was selected as one of the six Scotland replacements for the match against Ireland in Dublin. Although the selectors were criticized for including a player with such a dreadful list of injuries and so little match practice, I did give the team cover as a goal kicker in the event of Peter Dods being injured.

As it transpired, none of the five players I might have replaced was injured, and I watched the full match from the grandstand along with the other replacements. In the evening, everyone associated with the win – players, replacements, coach, selectors, committee men, the medical team – all happily joined together to celebrate that historic night, although inevitably it can never be quite so glamorous for the replacements as it is for the actual players. However, the following month, I was able to put everything into perspective on the day of the Grand Slam confrontation with France.

I sat in the stand in my tracksuit, willing Scotland to win, impervious to the fact that I was missing out myself on the one truly supreme moment of triumph for Scottish rugby since 1925. I watched the early war of attrition in the first half principally as a fanatically keen and proud Scotsman but I also felt supercharged with the adrenalin pumping through my body in the knowledge that I might conceivably be given a final opportunity to fight for Scotland's cause at Murrayfield. The moment of truth came as half-time approached. Both Peter Dods our full back and Roger Baird on the left wing had been injured and received treatment. I was summoned from the grandstand and told to warm up in the car park behind the main stand at Murrayfield. I had loosened up properly and stretched every muscle in an intensive ten

13

minute burst of activity when the chairman of the selectors, Ian MacGregor, called me into the tunnel and more or less told me I would be going on at half-time for either Dods or Bairds, whoever was the more seriously injured. During the last few minutes before the half-time whistle I stood beside Ian MacGregor, furiously running on the spot on a rubber mat just a few yards from the pitch.

The funny thing was that I had always been a very confident player and had usually performed pretty well against the French. Part of me was aching to burst out of the tunnel and onto the pitch so I could have a go against France and share in a moment of history. Yet part of me was apprehensive because of the importance and significance of the occasion, especially in the knowledge that I had only played a handful of games in the previous six months. I was fully aware that there was a distinct possibility that my lack of match practice and match fitness might let down the rest of the team, our legion of loyal supporters and indeed the whole nation. When the message came back during half-time that both players considered themselves fit enough to continue – I can say this with my hand on my heart – my instant reaction was actually relief. Of course it would have been great to have gone on and kicked the winning penalty in injury time, but I had experienced a momentary flutter of self doubt and apprehension warming up in the tunnel which brought home to me the possibility that I might let Scotland down. I realized as I clambered back up to my seat in the stand that the only thing that really mattered on 17 March 1984 was that Scotland beat France to win the Championship.

I had had a wonderful treasure chest of memories over the years and had no regrets. I had topped the half century of caps, captained my country and been on three British Lions tours. I had had good games and bad games over twelve exciting seasons and, through rugby, I had experienced just about every emotion known to man. I was immensely proud that day as I joined the victorious team in the changing room afterwards. Standing in the home dressing room at Murrayfield for the very last time, as I knew I was, I think I was almost as thrilled as anyone in the room. But while I drank some champagne and joined in the celebrations, I also wondered how long it might be before such a scene would be repeated. I caught sight of Alister Campbell, the new lock forward in the opposite corner of the room, and I must confess I wondered if he really appreciated how kind the good fairy had been to him. In his first two games for Scotland he had been in a winning Triple Crown side and a triumphant Grand Slam side. Did he know it would get worse before it got better? Guys had been playing their hearts out in navy blue jerseys since 1938 to win a Triple Crown and since 1925 to win a Grand Slam. There had been 59 years of blood, sweat, toil and tears. In his first two matches, in the space of a month, he had fulfilled every Scottish rugby player's dream. It had been a great day for the team, for the selectors and for the coach, Jim Telfer, and I was delighted for them all.

It was wonderful to be Scottish in March 1984 and as I look back now at the ups and downs, the good times and the not so good times of all my years in Scottish rugby, it is gratifying to recall that in retiring from centre stage I was able to go out, admittedly standing in the wings, sharing in the reflected glory of the ultimate triumph as the curtain came down on Scotland's most memorable post-war performance.

In looking back on my career the most curious fact is that throughout childhood and early schooldays all my dreams and ambitions revolved around playing for Scotland at Hampden Park and not Murrayfield. Born in September 1951, exactly five years later I went to James Gillespie's Boys School in Edinburgh, which was a soccer-playing school in the winter and which concentrated on athletics and cricket in the summer. There was no rugby. Until I left Gillespie's at the age of 12 I was a soccer fanatic and not only did I play in the school team in each of my last three years there, I lived, ate and slept soccer every moment of my life. I was a right wing in those good old days of wingers, inside forwards and a centre forward, and because I was reasonably quick and had a good shot I used to score a lot of goals.

I lived in a part of Edinburgh called Liberton and every day after school I would rush home, change into my football gear and join my friends from the nearby school to kick a ball about until it got dark in the winter or our parents rounded us up in the summer. I was soccer daft and played football seven days every week for 52 weeks of the year. My first brush with success on the games field came in my second last year at Gillespie's when we won the local school league for the first time in living memory. I recall thinking at that time that to bridge the gap between the dizzy heights of the invincible Gillespie's Under-12 All Stars and helping Scotland to win the World Cup I would have to sign for one of the big city First-Division sides. For as long as I can remember I have been a Heart of Midlothian supporter. In the late 1950s and early 1960s they had some great players and my sporting heroes were stars like Dave Mackay, Willie Bauld and Johnnie Hamilton, not the brilliant rugby players of the day such as Arthur Smith and Ken Scotland. I am quite convinced that the six years or so that I devoted to playing soccer stood me in good stead throughout my rugby career.

In the summer I managed to find a place in the school cricket side as an all-rounder and also found time to sprint in the school athletics team. It was through athletics that I first encountered the outstanding Heriot's school sporting facilities at Goldenacre when Gillespie's pitched up for the contest. Compared to all the other training fields I had seen at Edinburgh schools these stood out as really special, and from that initial introduction to Goldenacre I determined that Heriot's would be the school for me.

The following term, when I arrived there, I was confronted with a straight choice between cross-country running and rugby, and because I have always preferred a team game to an individual sport, I opted for rugby. On the first Tuesday I was put in a trial match with all the other novices, but by the end of the afternoon I had managed to gain promotion to the trial for the top two teams in the first year of the senior school.

I had scored a few tries in the novices imitation of a rugby match, but now I was chucked in with a group of boys who had three distinct advantages over me. They had played rugby before for at least a year, they all knew each other and, even more important, they had a basic knowledge of the laws of the game. No sooner was I on the pitch bursting with energy and enthusiasm, raring to show my paces, than I was sent off. From the kick-off we launched an attack and one of our team scored. I jumped up and down with excitement and followed the accepted behaviour of any self-respecting soccer player brought up in the true Tynecastle tradition. I applauded heartily, rushed over to the hero of the moment and doubtless hugged and kissed the startled youth on both cheeks. The games master, Donald Hastie, ordered me off the field; the only time, I hasten to add, such a humiliation has happened to me in 20 years. He explained that rugby players did not behave in that manner. I never forgot that lesson which was tucked away in the back of my mind for the rest of my career. I hope that Donald Hastie noted that whenever I scored a try or kicked a penalty in an international, I never jumped up and down, shook the hands of my team mates or rushed around kissing anyone. In the mould of Rudyard Kipling, Hastie taught me the cruel lesson that should I meet with triumph and disaster I should treat those two impostors just the same. I like to think that outwardly I showed no great emotion on the rugby field whether I had just scored a try or given one away, and I am delighted that good manners and generous sportsmanship have always been an integral part of the whole ethos and ideology of rugby.

By the second Saturday of term I had convinced the games master I was unlikely to further embarrass the

school, and I made my rugby debut at centre threequar-
ter for the school team of my age group. Although I
played a handful of games at full back and on the wing in
my last two years at school, I spent almost all of my six
years at Heriot's playing in the centre. I was very
fortunate to be educated at a school like Heriot's with
such a fine rugby playing tradition. That tradition was
built round splendid and dedicated coaches epitomised
by the likes of Gibby Galloway and Willie Waitt. They
will always remain in my memory for their gentle
guidance and enthusiasm. I think versatility is an
important quality and not only do I believe every
youngster should be encouraged to play soccer in his
formative years to acquire a basic ball sense, but I'm
glad that early in my senior career I was equally
competent performing at full back, in the centre or on the
wing. Soccer is a great training at school for future rugby
players, and I know that a lot of the skills which I
assimilated at Gillespie's were to prove extremely useful
throughout my career.

My interest in rugby flourished at Heriot's when I
made the 1st XV in my fourth year at school. The
highlight of that year was my first 'tour'. We flew over to
Dublin to play against Belvedere College. The match
ended in a 9–9 draw and I managed to kick all three
penalties. It would be nice to think that the locals in
Ireland that day would remember my kicking exhibition
as something rather special, but that is most unlikely as I
discovered they boasted a young ginger-haired lep-
rechaun in one of their younger sides at the time by the
name of Ollie Campbell who was beginning to acquire a
reputation as a pretty useful kicker!

In my fifth and sixth years I had the extremely happy
experience of playing in the centre for Edinburgh Schools
and also for the Scottish Schools. My first match for
Scottish Schools was against the Welsh at Cardiff Arms
Park in January 1969, and not for the only time in my
career, representing Scotland in Cardiff, we finished
second. We lost by 20 points to 9 to a Welsh Secondary

18

Schools side containing a string of future stars including winger John Bevan who scored two tries that day, Brynmor Williams at scrum half and Graham Price at prop. Our next match was in Edinburgh at Goldenacre against the English Schools and I was opposite Geoff Evans in the centre – five years later we were to tour South Africa together with the British Lions. Scotland won that match but the following season lost to both England and Wales. I relished that first taste of representative honours and all the peripheral paraphernalia which surrounds such an occasion, and with the game now in my blood I finally decided to concentrate on rugby rather than soccer when I left school and went up to Edinburgh University.

I have to confess that up to the time that I actually played for Scotland at senior international level, I had only been to Murrayfield twice as a spectator. Although I was involved in rugby at school I still tended to follow the fortunes of Hearts soccer team when they had home midweek matches at Tynecastle, and I even ventured occasionally during the holidays to see how the other half lived by crossing Edinburgh to Easter Road to watch Hibs. I know that if I had not gone to a rugby-playing senior school my ambition in life would have been to play soccer for Hearts or Hibs.

Sport was always destined to play a large part in my life because throughout my school days I lived for the two or three hours of daylight every afternoon after school when I could swim, do athletics or play soccer, rugby, tennis, golf or whatever my friends happened to organize. I was never one of those children who could be amused or entertained with a good book or electric train set or indeed any indoor game. My mother still recalls that when most kids dropped their annual note to Santa Claus reminding him of the urgent desire and need for such essentials as a meccano set or Lego, a cowboy outfit or a machine gun, a bike or a game of Monopoly, I wrote for more practical presents like a new pair of boots, a tennis racquet, golf balls, a football or a cricket bat.

It is interesting to recount that much as I loved every moment playing as a kid in the streets or public parks in Edinburgh, I always had a competitive edge. Winning was not absolutely everything, but trying to win was, and although I like to think I have always been a good loser, even as a ten-year-old boy I played flat out at every sport to win. If a half a dozen of us turned up to play a game of soccer in the streets after school, we would play three-a-side with the rules invariably the same – five goals to half-time, with the first to eleven, not ten, being the winner because, traditionally, we had an extra goal for luck. This had the desired effect of delaying the assault on our homework by an extra few valuable minutes. That early instinctive desire to win has courted me all my life and nowadays, whether I'm playing touch rugby in training or a game of snooker or darts, I try my hardest to win. I have become a bit of a golf buff in the summer and even a friendly game is enhanced for me by putting up a token prize of a golf ball for the winner.

The competitive element is inbuilt in my character, and whether turning out for Heriot's, Scotland or the British Lions my team-mates will confirm that I talk non-stop during a game trying to generate interest and encourage people to do their very best with my own infectious kind of enthusiasm.

The greatest empathy with my own uncompromising attitude may undoubtedly be found in the borders of Scotland because, as in the valleys of Wales or the great provinces of New Zealand, rugby is the single most important sport by a very long way. In the borders, it is rugby first, other sports nowhere. In consequence I did toy with the idea of playing for Melrose because I became friendly with two Melrose lads in the Scottish Schoolboys team – Jim Henderson and George Elliot. At their invitation I went down from Edinburgh to play in a seven-a-side tournament for Melrose and this initial contact with border rugby made a deep impression on me. Border rugby was, and still is, better organized, more dedicated and more important than the game in the big cities of Edinburgh and Glasgow. In the borders everyone is interested in rugby – mothers, fathers, aunts, uncles, professional people, the working classes, the idle rich and the unemployed. Town and village life revolves round the fortunes of the local XV. It was a decent Melrose side in those days and we won all the four tournaments which we entered in the spring of 1970.

When I was selected at the start of the next season for Melrose, I had to make the decision between playing for Heriot's, Melrose or Edinburgh University. Living and studying in Edinburgh it was not that difficult a decision, and I settled for the easiest and, I am certain in retrospect, the best option – I chose Heriot's. I felt a sense of loyalty to show an initial allegiance to my old school. They were a more convenient choice than Melrose and a much stronger side than the University. It was a decision which I have never regretted because I have enjoyed 15 wonderful years in their 1st XV playing a marvellous brand of attractive, running rugby for one of the finest clubs in Britain. I can honestly say that when I wake up on a Saturday morning now I look forward to an afternoon in a Heriot's jersey every bit as much as I did as a bright-eyed, bushy-tailed, fresh-faced youth in 1970.

Having established myself in the Heriot's side, I divided my energies during the next three years between rugby and the pursuit of academic excellence at Edinburgh University – or to phrase it more accurately, the desperate scramble to achieve 50½ per cent in all university examinations. As my rugby career blossomed with regular games for Edinburgh in the interdistrict championship, Scottish trials, Scotland 'B' selection and, by my final year as a student, for the full Scotland side, my studies inevitably began to suffer. Furthermore, after two years of studying geology, I worked out that the end product of an Honours degree in that particular field of activity would leave me with the stark choice between life on an oil-rig in the North Sea or prospecting for gold in the Australian desert. Neither seemed the perfect catch-

21

ment area for the Scottish rugby selectors, and with that in mind I switched to geography in my final year. Along with geography I had to glean a working knowledge in science studies, computer programming and statistics, and I was very fortunate that my girlfriend, Audrey, was following a similar course. It struck me as an unnecessary luxury for both of us to attend every single lecture, so we developed the perfect division of labour whereby Audrey fulfilled all the academic obligations and I managed to fit in a lot of midweek rugby.

I played in every conceivable invitation match and on a regular basis for a team called the Edinburgh Wednesday Club. It was a side made up of students who played for their old school teams on a Saturday like Heriot's, Watsonians, or Edinburgh Academicals and who wanted a game of rugby in midweek. These matches were enormous fun and were an entertaining extension to the philosophy of the famous Barbarians club. The Baabaas have an unwritten rule that you do not kick outside your own 22; the Wednesday Club, showing commendable ambition, had an unwritten rule that you do not kick. They were fast and furious games which I remember now with great affection. My three years at Edinburgh University were among the happiest of my life and I'm delighted to recount that the excellent working partnership which I struck up with Audrey in our final year together as geography students did not end when we both graduated in 1973. We married the following year and our family now comprises Jennie, Sara and Nicola; potentially, three conscientious geography students well worth befriending by three future rugby players.

2

Launching an International Career

I went up to University in October 1970. Later that season I played my first few big representative games for Edinburgh on the wing in the District Championship. I spent most of that season for Heriot's either in the centre or on the wing because Colin Blaikie, who won eight caps for Scotland, was at full back. However, when Colin was injured or unavailable I was switched to full back, and after he retired at the end of that season I became the regular full back for Heriot's for the next 14 years. Even though I was relatively new to the game of rugby, and pretty raw and naïve when it came to the hurly burly of club matches, I realized from the very outset that the full back had enormous potential to be the most exciting and rewarding position on the field. My thoughts were perhaps shaped by some of the charismatic characters who had stamped their authority on the game at that time; players like J. P. R. Williams of Wales and Pierre Villepreux of France whose enterprising approach and general attitude confirmed my early impressions that the recipient of the number 15 jersey was not primarily, or solely, the last line of defence but also the first line of attack.

I have to confess that right from the beginning of my career I tended to place much more emphasis on attacking than defending. Because of my adventurous attitude to the game I have made some dreadful mistakes in the heat of battle. Nevertheless, I have always stuck to the simple philosophy that if I gave away three tries attempting to open up from my own goal line but managed to score, or help to score, four tries at the other end, then I was collecting a bonus point on the afternoon. I would rather have that approach than save ten tries with heroic defence but never take any risk to launch an attack.

The following season I became established at full back in both the Heriot's and Edinburgh sides, and I was fortunate that at that time in my new position there was only one good player challenging for the Scotland team. Colin Blaikie and Iain Smith, both incidentally former Heriot's schoolboys, had dropped out of consideration, and the man in possession was Arthur Brown of Gala. He played against England at the end of the 1971 season and in every international in 1972. I had managed to edge my way into contention with selection on the wing in the Scottish trial in December 1971, and for the final match of that season against England in March 1972 I was made a member of the Scotland squad and began my sojourn in the big time just as I was to end it 12 years later – sitting on the bench as a replacement.

Funnily enough, my abiding memory of that first important weekend was spotting the peripheral luxuries with which newcomers to the squad were greeted as part of the initiation ceremony. I received a gleaming new pair of Adidas boots and an Adidas tracksuit. To conform with the thinking of the Scottish Rugby Union at that time everyone had to pay 50 pence for each of the articles; a gesture which somehow was supposed to safeguard our amateur ideals. It seemed a small sum to part with and it was not really the actual goods which meant so much to me as the status and elevated position that these trappings automatically heralded.

The highlight of the first half of the next season was the visit of the All Blacks on a 30 match tour of Britain, Ireland and France. They had notched up two wins in warm-up games in Canada before they arrived in Britain, and they began with another handsome victory

against the Western Counties at Gloucester. However, I
was soon reassured that they were not invincible because
they lost to Llanelli, and before they reached Hawick at
the end of November for their first game in Scotland they
had also lost to the North-West Counties in Workington.
I was not eligible for selection for the Rest of Scottish
Districts side because Edinburgh and Glasgow were due
to put out a combined team against the tourists four days
before the Scotland international at Murrayfield, and
this meant that no one from the two major cities could
play in the match at Hawick.

My interest in that match was partly to catch a first
ever glimpse of the mighty All Black team, and partly to
monitor the performance of Arthur Brown at full back for
the Scottish Districts. Arthur had played for the combined Scotland and Ireland side against England and
Wales in October at Murrayfield in a match to celebrate
the Scottish centenary season, and I had been made
aware of how close I was getting to a cap by the fact that
I was on the replacement bench for that particular
extravaganza. My vague memories of that day were
meeting Willie John McBride for the first time and being
impressed by the sheer bulk and stature of the man; also
sitting next to Gareth Edwards on the bench; and the
famous moment in the match when Peter Brown, the
captain of the Scotland and Ireland side and a remarkable character, called for the ball at a kick-off – when it
arrived, instead of catching it, he headed it directly into
touch. It was the outrageous act of an outrageous player,
but it was the sort of unorthodox touch that I thoroughly
enjoyed.

Arthur Brown played well that afternoon in a handsome victory over England and Wales, but he had the
dreadful misfortune to break a leg in the match against
the New Zealanders at Hawick, and I realized I was
being propelled pretty rapidly towards my first cap. The
All Blacks won that match, beat Wales the following
Saturday and won their next three games to arrive at
Murrayfield for the Scotland match with a very im-

25

pressive record. I should have been confident of selection as I had spent a year as travelling reserve, but in November I had been picked for the Scotland 'B' game against France 'B' and had not played well. I was worried that I might have blown my chance because the conditions were wet and windy. The pitch was completely open to the elements which, in the north of Scotland in November, are not usually compatible with the ambitions of a young running full back trying to make his name. The choice of Inverness was the culmination of a geographical battle of wits, a sort of orienteering war of attrition being waged between the respective unions of Scotland and France. After being led a merry dance to remote pitches in the middle of the hinterland of France on our two previous cross-channel excursions – somewhere half-way up the Alps on one occasion and, apparently, half-way up the Pyrenees on the other – the Scottish Rugby Union had boldly responded in kind.

I did not have a happy afternoon in Inverness, and when the selectors announced the trial teams a fortnight before the Scotland–New Zealand clash I found myself in the junior side with David Aitchison, the man who replaced Arthur Brown when he was injured at Hawick, in the senior side. Fortunately, by half-time of that trial I had broken out of defence several times with long jinking runs and kicked a few goals, and so was promoted to the senior side for the second half. The trial continued to go well for me after half-time, but near the end I hurt a knee badly and, although I finished the final five minutes of the game, the leg stiffened up that night.

The Scotland side was announced a couple of days later, and I was the proudest man north of the Border when I learned that I had won my first international cap; but I was also the most worried because my knee was still very painful and there were real doubts that I would be fit in time. After the announcement of the team right up to the Thursday before the match, I took up almost permanent residence at the Chalmers Hospital where the orthopaedic surgeon, Jimmy Thomson, and his team of

26

physiotherapists treated me two or three times a day in a furious effort to get the leg right. By the time the squad assembled on the Thursday I had enough movement in the joint to run at almost full pace but I knew that the knee was still not 100 per cent right. However, I was bursting with excitement and enthusiasm and reckoned that if I poured a crate of liniment onto the offending joint to anaesthetize it, and relied on the inevitable adrenalin to pump the blood round my body at the speed of light, the drama of the occasion would enable me to forget my problems and concentrate on the matter in hand. The selectors put me through a fitness test which comprised mostly of running, and as that particular form of exertion was well within my pain threshold, I managed to survive.

Ironically enough, having successfully persuaded the doctors and the Scottish Rugby Union that I was fit, I was caught out by the photographers who asked if they could take a photo of me, the new cap, with the captain, Peter Brown. They wanted us to squat down and smile at the array of cameras, but when I was half-way down into the squat position I realized that the pain in my knee was such that there was not the remotest possibility of me successfully meeting their request. However, I sensed that that sort of knowledge should not be shared amongst too many people, so in great haste I lowered myself into a relatively comfortable position, half kneeling with one hand on Peter Brown and the damaged leg almost straight behind me. I then asked the photographers to take their photos as fast as possible, saying I wanted to practise my goal kicking and it was already beginning to get dark. They duly obliged, and before anyone became too suspicious the ordeal was over and I was hurrying back after a couple of pots at goal, to the physio's healing hands.

By the Saturday the knee was much better and I felt confident that I would be able to do everything flat out. The physio confirmed that I had regained full movement and there was virtually no risk of letting down the rest of

27

the team. As it transpired, I took a lot of knocks in the match and I was pretty bruised and sore afterwards, but the knee presented no problem at all during the game. The fact that I was preoccupied with the knee all through the week helped to keep my mind off the match to a large extent, although I have never been a nervous type of person, so even for my first cap against the greatest rugby nation in the world I was not especially overawed. I was excited at the prospect of playing for Scotland at Murrayfield and was naïve enough at that early stage in my career not to appreciate just how consistently good the All Blacks were.

I remember feeling immense relief when the Friday training session finished. Having survived that, nothing stood between me and my first cap. All those games in the public park near my home in Liberton, when I had represented Scotland in my mind's eye, were part of every schoolboy's dream world but nothing has given me more pleasure in my life than turning fantasy into reality and running onto the field at Murrayfield nine days before Christmas in 1972 – it was the best possible present and it was a day, a game and an occasion to savour for ever.

Apart from the result, everything conspired to make it a day to remember. The weather was superb for the time of year, bright, dry, hardly a breath of wind and 70,000 supporters willing Scotland to a first ever victory over New Zealand. Interestingly enough, I have always felt more self-conscious performing in a mickey mouse match in front of three men and a dog than I have in front of a capacity crowd on international day, and as a firm believer in the fact that rugby is an amateur game to be played for fun and enjoyment, I have always relished the big occasion. Looking back now, I can see that I ought to have felt apprehensive and suffered an outbreak of butterflies – especially in view of how many outstanding world-class players were crammed into that New Zealand side. Joe Karam was a lively full back, Bryan Williams and Grant Batty were two of the best wings around, Bruce Robertson was just about the finest centre in the world, and Sid Going was a genius of a scrum half. With forwards like Ian Kirkpatrick, Alex Wylie, Peter Whiting and Tane Norton they were a formidable team.

Not fully appreciating all this, I had the precocious effrontery to break out of defence early on and set off on a long run down the blind side. I was fortunate that I caught some high kicks in the first 20 minutes of the game, unleashed mostly by Sid Going, and coping successfully with these gave me the confidence to play my natural attacking game throughout. On two or three occasions in the first half I counter-attacked from loose opposition kicks, and I joined our three-quarter line in attack to add a new dimension to Scottish tactics. The previous two or three Scottish full backs had been very steady, safe players, but not since the days of Stewart Wilson and Ken Scotland had Scotland had a running man at the back.

Even in that first international I took some horrendous risks but, perhaps because nobody was anticipating it, most of my bravado seemed to succeed. I was pretty quick for a full back and could wriggle out of trouble if necessary, and I was so unothodox by recent Scottish standards that no one knew what I was going to do next. It was a pleasant feeling, and for my first taste of the big time it was a fantastic experience.

For all Scotland's brave running and attacking, we were six points down at half-time – Sid Going had put Kirkpatrick away on the blind side of a scrum for a try which Karam converted. I landed a long-range penalty early in the second half, but then Bruce Robertson with a glorious swerving run and delightfully accurate kick made a try for Grant Batty. With our pack playing particularly well, we hit back in the last quarter. Ian McGeechan dropped a goal, and I banged over a penalty from near the half-way line to leave the All Blacks clinging on precariously to a one-point lead as the match went into injury time. Scotland were within one score of making history, and with only a few minutes remaining we had to attack. I stood up in the three-quarter line throughout that final flurry to make the extra man, but in a passing move around midfield a long, speculative overhead pass from Alastair McHarg was intercepted by Sid Going who ran 50 yards to score and clinch victory. To try and win we had had to take risks in those dying moments and, because I was up in the line, once Going intercepted the ball he was bound to score because he had no one to beat. But if he had not made the interception we would have had an overlap and might well have scored at the other end. It was as close, exciting and dramatic as that.

My immediate reaction was a mixture of disappointment at losing and delight that it had been such a good game. Also I had had the opportunity to indulge myself in several long sorties out of defence. It would have been wonderful to have won, but it was still a very enjoyable match, and I was relieved that my knee had survived and I had begun my international career with a pretty respectable performance.

On the strength of my performance against New Zealand I kept my place in the Scottish side for the rest of the season. The various matches in the Five Nations Championship, which ended with all five countries level with two wins and two defeats each, are chronicled elsewhere, but I do not want to leave my first season of international rugby and Scotland's centenary year without due reference to the celebrations at the end of the season. On the last day of March, I played for Scotland against a select team under the grand title of the Scottish Rugby Union President's XV. Despite a wet and windy day, the match produced a feast of good rugby and a 27–16 win for Scotland. That sort of festive occasion was the ideal platform for a lively Scottish back division to cut loose against a scratch side comprising players from Australia, New Zealand, South Africa and France with little time to prepare properly. I spent the whole afternoon joining the three-quarter line, and enjoyed the luxury of initiating several long-range attacks from full back, two of which resulted in tries in the first half for Dave Shedden and Drew Gill, our wings.

The following Saturday I was back at Murrayfield again for the final spectacular act of the centenary season – the special World Seven-a-Side tournament. This was a superb day's entertainment, and it has always been a major surprise to me that this brilliantly original idea has never been repeated. Sevens is a great spectator sport in almost any circumstances, and to bring the very best rugby players in the world together for a really fast-moving bonanza seemed a clever concept which I felt Scotland should have repeated every three or four years. The tournament was full of surprises with the best two sides, England and Wales, both in groups B, and Australia, who were to become the outstanding sevens exponents in the 1980s, unable to win a single game in group A. Scotland's only win was against Australia, for the host nation lost to both New Zealand and the ultimate group A winners, Ireland.

I failed to make the Scotland seven but was picked at centre for the Scottish President's seven along with Jim Renwick, Dougie Morgan and Dave Shedden. Our two props were two great Springbok loose forwards, Jan Ellis and Piet Greyling, but they were at a severe disadvantage because the abbreviated form of rugby is hardly ever played in South Africa. They were also taken aback at the training session on the Friday which was conducted by our coach for the weekend, Jim Telfer. It was the most punishing session I ever experienced in my career, and seemed to last for several hours, so that we were all shattered by the end. We managed to beat France who, like the New Zealanders and the South Africans, found the game quite foreign to them, but we lost to both England and Wales.

The England side reached the final by beating Wales 24–10, and that was a remarkably good performance when you consider the team that represented Wales that afternoon. The forwards were Mervyn Davies, John Taylor and J. P. R. Williams which should have guaranteed them a bit of everything – line-out and kick-off possession, scrum ball, and, as a bonus in the open, three gifted runners and passers. The backs did not look all that bad either – Gareth Edwards at scrum half, Phil Bennett at fly half, Gerald Davies in the centre and J.J. Williams on the wing. Having scored 66 points in beating the Scottish Rugby Union President's side and France, they came unstuck against England because their forwards failed to win enough ball for their outstanding backs. The English triumvirate of Fran Cotton, John Gray and Andy Ripley had the better of the exchanges against the Welsh trio in that crunch match, and with Steve Smith at scrum half controlling and orchestrating the whole show, and Keith Fielding, the fastest man in rugby boots in the world at that time, running in tries galore on the wing, England deservedly reached the final.

They had only a brief break between beating Wales and taking on an Irish team in the final who had had the best part of an hour to recover from their last match in group A. The fact is that Ireland had only two top-notch sevens exponents – Mike Gibson at scrum half and Fergus Slattery – and although they lost narrowly 22–18 to England they were a very makeshift side who did well to reach the final at all.

Exactly a month after the World Sevens I played for the Public Schools Wanderers select side in the Middlesex Sevens in front of a capacity crowd of 60,000 at Twickenham. We would almost certainly have won that competition but the aeroplane bringing Fergus Slattery over from Ireland was late and he arrived at Twickenham just 20 minutes before our first-round tie. We had already managed to rustle up a replacement after a desperate search, and Fergus had to adopt the role of spectator throughout that afternoon. Good victories over Wasps and Rosslyn Park were followed by a last-minute win over Saracens as we fought back from 16–0 down at half-time to win 18–16. The final against London Welsh was generally reckoned to be the best

32

since the war, and the *Daily Telegraph* rugby writer,
Rupert Cherry, claimed it was the most exciting of the 47
he had witnessed over the years.

The lead changed hands repeatedly before London
Welsh eventually won 24–22. I played in the centre with
the half-backs – now the well-known BBC pairing of
Nigel Starmer-Smith and Ian Robertson – using their
experience to give myself and Keith Fielding the room,
as well as the half overlaps, to run in the tries. I must say
that I had been very disappointed at Fielding's reluctance to do much running in the early rounds, and I had
assumed that he was saving himself for a special effort in
the final. In fact he did not offer much in the final either,
and Robertson and myself seemed to have to do all the
running. Right at the end, though, I made a half-break,
and the ball reached Fielding on the half-way line to give
him a clear run to the line. As he set off for what would
have been the winning try, the referee, Geoff Fenn, blew
his whistle for a forward pass. Afterwards television
showed, and Mr Fenn admitted, that the pass was not
forward but it had been a fabulous tournament and it
was a fitting climax that, in his final appearance in
Britain, the London Welsh, Wales and British Lions
captain, John Dawes, should receive the trophy. With
gifted sevens players like Dawes, Billy Hullin, John
Taylor and J. P. R. Williams, the London Welsh were a
formidable club team, and I have always felt that it was
to their great credit later that year that, when some of the
London clubs objected to a select side like Public Schools
Wanderers being allowed to play in the Middlesex
Sevens, the Welsh spoke up in favour of our inclusion. It
was a magnanimous gesture which came to nothing as
new, clumsy and petty rules were inaugurated just to
make sure invitation clubs like Public Schools Wanderers and the Barbarians could never again play in the
biggest sevens competition in the Northern Hemisphere.

I would like to finish this discussion of seven-a-side
rugby by saying that although the Twickenham tournament in 1973 was one of the highlights of my whole

career, the best, most lavish and most glamorous tournament in the world is the annual Cathay Pacific Hong Kong Bank Sevens in Hong Kong every spring. It comes nearest to the Scotland centenary sevens in concept and composition, and each year it is becoming closer to a world sevens competition. With the advent of the first Rugby Union World Cup at 15-a-side scheduled for May 1987 in Australia and New Zealand, I would love to see the Cathay Pacific Sevens raised that final extra level to an annual world cup for sevens. Already Australia, New Zealand and 14 or so other countries in the Pacific Basin send their full international sevens sides picked by their national selectors. America, Canada and Argentina have followed suit in recent years, but the Five Nations countries have held back in isolation from giving it full status. The Barbarians sent a very powerful side in 1981 and 1982, and I went twice with the Co-Optimists from Scotland in 1980 and 1981. In the last two years the French Barbarians, the Irish Wolfhounds, Crawshays, the Welsh invitation team, and the Public Schools Wanderers have all sent outstanding sides packed with top-class, famous internationals who are all well-known players from the Five Nations Championship.

I would like to think that it is only a matter of time before each of the home unions sends a full international seven to Hong Kong. In my view, the Cathay Pacific tournament is the most exotic, spectacular and popular rugby event of its kind, and it is staggering to play on one of the few green oases in the middle of the most densely populated concrete jungle in the world. It is strange that a pitch surrounded by hundreds of giant skyscrapers should attract each year so many of the world's top rugby players. It was a real eye-opener for me to admire the athletic dexterity of the Fijians, the sheer genius of the Australians, the ingenuity of the Japanese, the blood-curdling ferocity of the Western Samoans and the total mastery of the game's basic skills by such unlikely sides as Korea and Malaysia. The sheer lack of ballast means that the majority of the countries in the Pacific Basin are at a severe disadvantage when they come up against any of the international board countries because they can never match the height, weight and strength of the forwards in Australasia or Britain, but at least in the less physically abrasive game of sevens they can display their natural talents. The whole week of the competition is crucial to the development of the game in these countries because it allows a wide cross-fertilization of ideas and, in the best possible surroundings and most friendly and pleasant atmosphere, the hopes and dreams of world rugby's Lilliputians are carefully fostered and encouraged.

The grass roots of the game are carefully being nurtured once a year in the nether regions of the most far-flung countries in the Southern Hemisphere. The players from sides like the Solomon Islands and Singapore return to spread the gospel in their clubs at home, and I believe the standard is improving every year. If the brutal truth be told, the international board do not do all that much to encourage and help the emerging countries where rugby union is a relatively new game. Admittedly it is a mammoth task, but this is all the more reason for the four home unions to send not just the occasional video tape and coaching pamphlet to the likes of Papua New Guinea and Thailand but their best players each year to the sevens in Hong Kong. That means the international sides of Scotland, England, Ireland and Wales. These sevens are where the East meets the West, the Occidental is confronted by the Oriental, and rugby is the common bond linking inextricably a host of different nations, cultures, creeds and backgrounds for seven magical days in the magnificent Hong Kong Hilton – one of the very best hotels I have stayed in on my many travels. I can vividly remember on my second visit in 1981 meeting a suave, bearded flanker from Sri Lanka called Angelo Wickremaratne who was proudly clutching some reports from his local Colombo daily newspaper from the previous year's competition. These showed him tackling John Rutherford and me in the match between the Co-Optimists and Sri Lanka. So it came about that the young man from a country I never even knew played rugby until that year was rubbing shoulders with seasoned internationals from the international board countries – and quite rightly so. In 1981 they had players like Hugo Porta of Argentina, the Ella brothers from Australia, Andy Ripley, Peter Wheeler, Clive Woodward from England, Roger Baird and Mike Biggar from Scotland, and many other famous players. There were also a hundred lesser-known players from lesser-known countries. The Cathay Pacific competition is developing and blossoming every year and doing wonders to spread the image and popularity of the game. I loved every moment of my two trips to Hong Kong, and it is singularly appropriate that such a fantastic, cosmopolitan gathering of the clans should take place in such a fantastic, cosmopolitan city.

3

The Auld Enemy

I played in ten Calcutta Cup matches altogether, but I think the first one in 1973 was in many ways the most interesting partly because it was my first, partly because it was almost as close as I was ever destined to get to a Triple Crown success, but also because the Scottish selection and performance ranked amongst the most controversial in the 1970s. After a narrow defeat by France by just three points in Paris we beat both Wales and Ireland at Murrayfield before setting off in pursuit of the Holy Grail at Twickenham in the middle of March. In scoring two tries to nil against Wales I think it was generally agreed we deserved our win and there was a tremendous feeling of optimism in the dressing room after a thrilling victory over Ireland by 19 points to 15. We were happy in the knowledge that we were just one game away from our first Triple Crown since 1938. The one dark cloud which cast an air of despondency over the initial euphoria was the loss of our captain Ian McLauchlan with a cracked fibula shortly before half-time of the Irish match.

Even those of us with no great medical background realized that a cracked fibula was a delicate way of describing a broken leg, and we knew that people who suffered a broken leg one Saturday were very unlikely to captain their country in an international three weeks later. In the event we were all wrong because McLauchlan did play at Twickenham but in retrospect in my opinion it was the wrong decision and was partially, but certainly not wholly, responsible for our defeat.

The stark truth of the matter is that several of our pack that afternoon were carrying injuries and although we might have been good enough to carry one passenger in the most important game that Scotland had played in many a long year, we were definitely not capable of taking on England with a pack which contained only two, perhaps three, forwards who were 100 per cent fit and free from injury.

After the match many people were critical of McLauchlan for playing within three weeks of breaking a leg and I suppose it was an unacceptably ludicrous risk to take. But I have to say that at the time there was a special aura about him as captain because he was one of the toughest players in contemporary rugby, and I know that I was pleased that weekend to learn that he would be playing. Having said that, my abiding memory of our changing room an hour before the match was not an inspiring sight. It resembled a bad day in a television hospital soap drama. To the best of my knowledge only two of our forwards were fit enough to run unaided onto the field of play. Half the pack had pain-killing injections for a variety of different ailments, and two were held together by strong bandages and strapping. I think the disappointing display of the pack was attributable to the accumulative effect of all the injuries which the forwards were trying to conceal and disguise between them. I can sympathize with each of them as individuals in hoping they would survive and be in the first Scottish Triple Crown winning side since the war, although each contributed to our demise. I think it is wrong to blame McLauchlan alone as an individual and prime suspect for the defeat simply because his particular injury was rather more obvious than those of the other invalids.

It is important to bear in mind that McLauchlan had made a tremendous impact that season in his new role as captain, and he had won the respect of the team for his forthright approach leading up to each international and his full-blooded example on the field during each match. His first game as captain was against Wales and he gave the most forceful, aggressive, inspirational team talks before a match that I have ever heard. It was a ruthless, unequivocal, highly charged gem of rhetoric delivered dramatically by a ruthless, unequivocal, highly charged man. It was the sort of address that Attila the Hun might well have delivered to his troops before he sacked a city, and needless to say this burst of emotional invective was not for the ears of children or those of a delicate constitution. There were one or two fairly mean individuals in that Scottish team and McLauchlan succeeded in whipping not only them but even the more faint-hearted and sensitive creatures into a lava of passion before letting them loose on the unsuspecting Welsh side which contained nine British Lions and had not lost to Scotland since 1967.

He produced a similar masterpiece of oratorical wizardry before our victory over Ireland and it would have been very demoralizing if he had not been there to lead us in the final leg of the quest for the Triple Crown at Twickenham. It is easy to say now that he was quite wrong to play but it is a vast oversimplification of a complex problem to claim that by playing with his damaged leg after three weeks without any proper training he let Scotland down and cost us the game, the Calcutta Cup and the Triple Crown. There were other reasons for our defeat, and if McLauchlan produced one of his least effective games for Scotland, there were a few other forwards on our side that day who could not be especially proud of their performance.

The English pack surprised all those who were not privy to our dressing room secrets and long casualty list by dominating the forward battle, and it would be wrong and a case of sour grapes to minimize their achievement. They raced to a commanding half-time lead of 8–0 with tries from Peter Squires and Peter Dixon, and if that was considered bad, there was worse to follow at the start of the second half. Peter Dixon helped himself to a second try when he rounded off a good peel from a line out and Tony Jordan converted it to make the score 14–0. In the last quarter of the match Gordon Brown came on as a replacement for Jock Millican who was concussed and gradually the Scottish pack clawed its way back into the game.

In the final pulsating 15 minutes we hit a real purple patch and, just for a moment, we threatened to defy the odds and win. Dougie Morgan kicked a penalty from near half-way and Billy Steele on the right wing scored two tries. Morgan missed the first conversion but I succeeded with the second from the touch-line to bring us right back to within one point at 14–13. However, right at the end, a high kick from Peter Preece bounced between Billy Steele and myself over our line and the nasty bounce resulted in the ball eluding both of us to allow Geoff Evans, following up in pursuit, to score. The mood in the changing room was very flat afterwards because we had lost a match virtually everyone in Scotland and England expected us to win. We had beaten England four times in succession prior to that game but, to a man, we would have swapped all four for a victory in 1973 to round off our centenary season in appropriate style.

The following year at Murrayfield we enjoyed our revenge in one of the best Calcutta Cup matches in which I had the pleasure to play. We quickly went 9–0 up when I kicked a penalty and converted a try by Wilson Lauder. A try by Fran Cotton and a penalty by Alan Old meant that at half-time we led by only two points. That advantage disappeared after consistent England pressure in the first part of the second half when, after a series of sweeping attacks, the final confrontation was Andy Ripley against Andy Irvine. It was a bit like a shoot-out in a Hollywood western as Ripley, arms and elbows and knees and boots flying in every direction bore down on me at full tilt. He had been unleashed by a long spin pass from scrum half Jan Webster, and I knew that if I made a mess of the tackle England would score and take the lead. Although I felt I had him properly lined up in my sights, I attempted to

40

take him too high – fatal against a player of Ripley's size. He burst through my tackle and managed to flick a pass out to Tony Neary in support and he scored. If the game had ended then I would have blamed myself for the defeat because, difficult though it is to tackle a fleet-footed awkward giant of 6 foot 5 inches and 16 stones, I ought to have knocked him over and saved the try.

Fortunately, I was given a chance to redeem myself soon after that disaster when I took the ball down the blind side from a ruck and jinked and zig-zagged my way past three or four defenders to score in the corner. I was sure that that try had won the game but with only a couple of minutes of proper time left England were back on the attack. The ball went loose in midfield inside our 25 and Colin Telfer kicked it upfield straight to the opposition full back, Peter Rossborough. Fifteen Scots on the pitch and another 40,000 or so in the ground watched helplessly as Rossborough dropped a goal from nearly 40 yards to put England in front 14–13. I was standing on our goal-line under the cross bar as I saw the ball drop over and I wanted to scream as I thought we had lost the match. It was infuriatingly frustrating to allow a game to slip out of reach in that manner but from the kick-off we launched our last-ditch offensive in a frantic effort to have the final word at the end of a fabulous game. We succeeded. The lead changed hands for the fourth time in the last 20 minutes when, in a moment of lost concentration, with no immediate danger, David Duckham played the ball from a hopelessly offside position to give us a penalty 40 yards out and near the right hand touch-line. It was an amazing aberration by such a player but it unquestionably cost England the Calcutta Cup that year. I felt incredibly confident teeing the ball up even though it was theoretically from the more difficult side of the field for a right-footed, round-the-corner kicker. I walked back feeling surprisingly free of tension and as I ran up I actually said to myself – this one is going over. The full-throated roar of the capacity crowd which greeted the kick confirmed that we had indeed stolen a dramatic victory, yet so confident was I that I was already running back ahead of my team-mates. As the flags were raised the final whistle went and I thought that even the English supporters would be glad they were there, despite the final result, because it had been so exciting and such a superb advertisement for rugby.

The match was featured recently on BBC Television's programme '100 Great Sporting Events', but if you think that everyone at Murrayfield that afternoon must have been purring with satisfaction just to have been there and seen such a special and thrilling match you are wrong. That game was the only time in my 50-odd caps for Scotland that my mother actually attended. After the match I tracked her down to see what her reaction was. Her first words were to ask me which side had won! She said it had been a pleasant enough day out but she would have enjoyed it much more if there had not been so many people there. She thought that in future she would just catch the highlights on television and that is exactly what has happened ever since. That was her first and last live rugby match. I knew she was not all that fanatical when I used to phone on a Monday after a Scotland team had been announced and I would tell her that I was off to play rugby in Paris at the weekend. She would gently enquire which team I was playing for and I would reply Scotland. There would be a slight pause and then she would tentatively ask which team we were playing against! The nice thing is that my mother has always enjoyed reading about my various exploits and has taken an interest in all the televised matches, and, in many ways, I am very relieved she has never been a rugby fanatic standing on the touch-line doling out advice. I have never been an enthusiastic fan of over-enthusiastic mums on the touch line.

The risk of floating on air or feeling smug and self-satisfied after kicking the winning goal on a Saturday in an international quickly evaporated when I went back into my office on the Monday. Working in a firm of chartered surveyors and estate agents I was asked to take a client to a commercial property in Leith, and making idle chit-chat we got round to talking about the match at Murrayfield on Saturday. He said that he had gone and was in raptures about what a good game it had been and how he was a really keen rugby man. After a brief silence he decided to continue the polite banter by mentioning that he had had a good seat on the half-way line and he inquired if I had bothered to go to the match and if I had, what sort of view did I have. I explained that I had been there and had had a good view pretty close to the action.

1975 was all too similar to 1973 as Scotland travelled to Twickenham for the last match of the season once again on the verge of a Triple Crown. Wins over Ireland by 20 points to 13 and Wales by 12 points to 10 left us seemingly with a Triple Crown at our mercy because England were a moderate side that season playing very moderate rugby. After a narrow defeat by Ireland, they had been well beaten by France, conceding four tries in the process, and Wales had destroyed them 20 points to 4 at Cardiff, running in three tries. In three internationals, nine tries had been scored against them and they had looked distinctly shaky all season. When the Scottish team assembled in London for the game we were far more confident than we had been for the same match two years previously and a huge contingent of supporters had made the pilgrimage to London for what promised to be a historic day. The same faithful kilted fans had traipsed back home with their sporrans flying at half-mast on too many trips in the past, but everyone agreed that the odds were firmly in our favour this time.

When ultimate success has been so long in coming, inevitably there is a fair amount of tension in the team and we relaxed on the Friday night with a visit to a comedy at one of the West End theatres. On the Saturday morning we left our hotel and travelled by coach to the Mitre Hotel at Hampton Court for an early lunch. After a light meal we adjourned to a special team room in the hotel. The chairman of the selectors, Dod

Burrell, joined us and began a vigorous pep talk on the importance of the result for Scottish rugby and every sports fan north of the border that day. He emphasized that in all his time in the game in the previous 30 years, there had never been a better opportunity to seize the elusive Triple Crown and bring lasting glory to our side that afternoon. He was half-way through a stirring address comparing any game against the English to war: we were the troops going over the top into battle fighting for our honour, for ourselves and for our families back home and we must take no prisoners, when suddenly a loud-speaker on the wall boomed out a message that a car was blocking a beer lorry and could the owner of the car with the following registration number please remove it at once.

All the players stared at the floor not quite sure where to look. A pregnant pause and then, the announcement over, Dod continued with his passionate, patriotic address recalling some of the great Scottish victories over the English down through the centuries but reminding us that this could be the greatest of them all. As he drew breath ready to continue in full throttle, the loud-speaker burst into voice again in a vain bid to find the errant car owner to allow the beer lorry to escape to his next port of call. Dod collected his thoughts and had just resumed his tirade against the English for the third time when he was deafened by the bellowing voice once again trying to sort out the problem of the illegally parked car and the impatient driver of the beer lorry. Every man has a breaking point and Dod's coincided with this third blaring interruption. He strode across the room, reached up to the loud-speaker half way up the wall and pulled it as hard as he knew how. After a furious 60-second skirmish he was triumphant. He ripped the speaker off the wall and, followed by an unsightly tangle of different coloured loose wires all over the place, he flung the offending and offensive object onto the floor. To make quite sure it was dead, he stamped on it and neatly linking this act of aggression to his theme for the day, he

44

proclaimed that was the way to treat English rugby players as well. Warming to this new angle to his sermon, he was once again in full flow when a second loud-speaker on the opposite wall recounted the latest position in the long-running saga of the trapped beer lorry and the inconsiderately parked car. Dod exploded. As he made a feverish rush towards the wall and we all anticipated observing the mutilation of a second speaker, one of the other selectors, Hamish Kemp, stood up and with a flick of his hand simply turned off the machine just as Dod arrived. It was such an outrageously straightforward act that Dod was left speechless but it certainly eased the tension as the whole team collapsed in laughter.

From the Mitre Hotel we set off for the ground but the shenanigans of Dod's team talk should have been an omen for us. We had hoped for good conditions, a firm pitch and a dry ball because we felt we had a decided edge in the backs. England had lost Duckham, Preece and Evans that year and we wanted to take them on in the three-quarters. The conditions, unlike 1973, were all against good rugby. It was wet and miserable. Dougie Morgan gave us the lead with a penalty but Neil Bennett replied in kind for England. Three-three at half-time. Morgan landed a second penalty early in the second half but then England took the lead for the first time when Peter Warfield punted the ball from about our ten-yard line over my head. In the soft conditions I anticipated the ball would not bounce all that high, and I moved back accordingly to intercept it as soon after it landed as I could manage. To my surprise, despite the state of the pitch, the greasy ball landed and then soared back over my head. Alan Morley booted it on over the line and in a desperate race Morley and I landed on the ball at almost exactly the same time, although I am quite certain in my own mind that I touched the ball down fractionally before Alan. I have to confess I was flabbergasted when the referee, Paddy D'Arcy, awarded the try. We trailed 7–6 with a quarter of an hour left and although we attacked most of that time we failed to secure the one score we needed for victory, for the Triple Crown, the Calcutta Cup and the share of the championship. Dougie Morgan missed two penalty kicks he would normally have got and Ian McGeechan was close with a snap left-footed drop at goal.

We knew we should have won that game but in a dour, unspectacular slog we failed to reproduce our better early-season form and England took their chances well. Without trying to belittle the English achievement we did suffer one severe blow both metaphorically and literally in the first five minutes when Nairn MacEwan had his jaw broken and we had no back-row forward replacement to take over. Lock forward Ian Barnes came on to play in the second row with Alistair McHarg dropping back to number eight and David Leslie moving from number eight to the flank. That one injury meant three actual changes which had an understandably disruptive influence on our pack. The scene in our dressing room after the match was as depressing as any I can remember. We had let a wonderful opportunity slip and I was never to be so close to a Triple Crown again.

The 1976 match at Murrayfield provides two very happy memories – the teams were presented to Her Majesty the Queen and Prince Philip before the game, and our victory that day was destined to be the last time I was to play in a winning Scottish side against the Auld Enemy. It began badly for us with the English fly half Alan Old making and then converting a try by Andy Maxwell. Old kicked two more penalties before half-time but, in between, I landed one for us and converted a sensational try by Alan Lawson very similar to the one Scotland scored against Wales in 1982. On that occasion Roger Baird counter-attacked from near his own line to initiate a move which ended with Ian Paxton scoring at the other end. In 1976 it was also our left wing, Dave Shedden, who set everything in motion by opening up from well inside his own 25-yard line and boldly running out of defence with the whole team in support and eventually Lawson touching down to score by the posts.

It was thrilling stuff and huge fun to be part of a side who had a sense of adventure and were prepared to take chances. All through my career my game has been based on attacking from anywhere at any time and I loved to be surrounded by players who shared these thoughts and ambitions.

I levelled the scores early in the second half with another penalty, and we gradually drew clear to win impressively with tries from David Leslie and a second from Alan Lawson. I added one conversion to give us a win by 22 points to 12, yet the funny thing is that we had actually had much more of the game the previous year at Twickenham when we lost. One of the great things about rugby is its unpredictability.

The following year was not a happy afternoon for Scotland. The selectors prematurely dropped McLauchlan in favour of Jim Aitken, and picked a most improbable blend in the back row of Wilson Lauder, Donald MacDonald and Alex Brewster. I felt sorry for Brewster, a most whole-hearted player, who was made the scapegoat for the forwards' collective failure when he was dropped for the next match. With England including the nucleus of what was to be their Grand Slam pack we were on a hiding to nothing. On a wet, windy, unpleasant afternoon their big pack destroyed us. They included Peter Wheeler and Fran Cotton in the front row, Bill Beaumont and Nigel Horton at lock and Peter Dixon and Roger Uttley in the back row and our forwards were outgunned and overwhelmed. Our only hope would have been if the England backs had been careless enough to throw the game away but they played very sensibly. Scrum half Malcolm Young linked well with his forwards to drive us back on our heels repeatedly and when the ball was moved it went no further than their big, strong fast centre, Charles Kent, the Oxford University Blue. He took umpteen crash balls in midfield and he took a devil of a lot of stopping. Once he exploded through everyone, scattering our centres, loose forwards, cover defence and full back in different directions to score a superb individual try. At other times when we did manage to stop him or at least slow him down, his team were quick in support and we were snuffed out of the game. We lost 26–6. It was a tactical triumph for England and, in truth, it could have been twice as big a defeat for us.

Another bad defeat in 1978 in the last match of the season left us the not-so-proud holders of the wooden spoon but we did much better in 1979 when, with a very inexperienced pack, including four guys in their first season of international rugby, we drew 7–7 at Twickenham. That was, up to that point, only the second time in my seven years for Scotland that we had avoided defeat in an away match.

The 1980 Calcutta Cup match was of special significance because it was the final game of the season and victory gave England not only the Grand Slam, but their first championship success since 1963. Without wishing to dwell too much on the English famine which lasted 17 years, I think it is worth mentioning that in view of all the senior players and the long list of so-called top clubs in England, the national side have done very badly for many years. Only once in the past 22 seasons up to 1985 have they won the Five Nations Championship. With dozens and dozens of good players involved in the game something must be radically wrong to finish up almost every season with a moderate international side.

From the outside looking in and from many conversations with the leading English players during my career it is abundantly clear that the whole system and structure of the game is in drastic need of a major overhaul. It is not simply a case of a little cosmetic surgery needed here and there. A painful and major operation is essential if new life is going to be instilled into the national team.

I have a rough idea of the bare bones of the two in-depth reports into the state of English rugby in recent years which were commissioned by the Rugby Football

Union. Many of the findings of the enquiry led by John Burgess in the early 1980s were strong echoes of the Mallaby report in the early 1970s. Both the final documents of Burgess and Mallaby, instead of being seized upon as the best hope of pointing English rugby in the right direction and giving them a reasonable chance of a decent future, have simply been allowed to gather dust. I do not have sufficient background knowledge to condemn the County Championship out of hand but it does seem highly implausible that there are enough top-quality players to spread them over 27 county teams – over 400 players in total – and unreasonable to expect such a feast of mediocrity to actually help the international selectors. Whatever the rights and wrongs of the County Championship there is scarcely any evidence at all to suggest that it has helped England come up with its best side year in and year out since 1964, and it is doubtful if the best players, spread so thinly through so many teams, receive any great benefit. No other major country has such a weak structure at the top.

In Wales, the selectors can pick their national side by watching half a dozen top sides battling it out every week in a fiercely competitive club system, just as they do in France. Scotland have an excellent and democratic league structure which involves the top 98 teams. The international XV is selected almost exclusively from the First Division sides. To secure the best concentration of the resources of a country, it is necessary to have a competitive club system. Furthermore, in Scottish rugby the cream of the available talent is condensed into the five district sides, Edinburgh, Glasgow, the South, the North-Midlands and the Anglos, allowing the selectors the best possible opportunity of evaluating individuals when the top 75 players eligible to play for Scotland are pitched against each other in a series of representative matches in the first half of the season. Ireland have a similar set up where the top 60 players are on view in the keenly contested inter-provincial championship featuring Ulster, Munster, Leinster and Connacht.

Only in England are the players left to try to fill the huge gap between club rugby, where there are no leagues and no incentives, and international rugby. Since the advent of coaching and the general improvement in standards of international rugby worldwide, it has proved an almost impossible task. My own view is that when England develops an official club league system involving the top clubs with promotion and relegation and they resurrect the divisional championship, they will win the Five Nations Championship very much more frequently than once every 20 years. With their best 60 players representing the North, the Midlands, the South and the South-west, the selectors would see the top players in action against each other at the highest level and they would have a much clearer idea of which players were up to playing international rugby and which were not. In recent years they have often discovered the failures actually on the field during internationals when it is too late. Very good club players often do not make the grade at international level and their weaknesses are far more likely to be exposed playing for the North of England against the Midlands than they are for Notts., Lincs. and Derby against Kent in the County Championship or for Richmond against Gosforth in a meaningless club match. Far too many players have won caps for England who are not good enough. These players would have been very unlikely to have succeeded in Scotland, Ireland, Wales or France – they would have been found out before winning a cap rather than in their first international. The sooner England make the necessary radical changes to their structure, the sooner they will take their rightful place in the scheme of things in the Five Nations Championship. Happily for them, most of the bad selections in the late 1970s had been weeded out by the end of the decade and in 1980 they were left with their best XV.

When they arrived at Murrayfield they were hot favourites to win the Championship for the first time since 1963, the Triple Crown for the first time since 1960 and the Grand Slam for the first time since 1957. Their pack was a perfect blend of solidity, line-out potential and speed. Fran Cotton, Peter Wheeler and Phil Blakeway were an outstanding front row and the best in Europe at that time even including the French. Bill Beaumont and Maurice Colclough complemented each other at lock ideally – they were both formidable scrummagers and excellent in the loose as well as in line-out play. John Scott and Roger Uttley were big, powerful men in the back row and also talented footballers, and Tony Neary on the open side was a brilliant, tearaway flanker. It was a great pack by any standards and these forwards were largely responsible for the team's success.

Steve Smith was exceptionally clever in playing to the pack and I thought their two most dangerous backs were Clive Woodward and John Carleton. It was my first match as captain of Scotland and I remember that from the moment both teams were announced I racked my brains to think of a cunning way we might win, but I couldn't come up with any plan of action worth half a chance. On paper their pack looked fully capable of demolishing our forwards in the scrums. On the day, particularly in the first half, that is exactly what happened. Just as I had feared, they cleaned us out in the line-out and my worst anxieties were realized as they raced to a 19–3 lead by half-time. At that point I was not too sure what an experienced international captain would have said to his beleagured troops, but this was my first attempt at the task and I said that our only hope of salvaging some honour from the match was to throw everything into attack and run whatever ball we did win in the second half no matter what the risks.

We had had the advantage of a stiff breeze in the first half, yet we had finished it sixteen points adrift. Realistically we were going to have to play out of our skins even to finish second. However, if we had concentrated on defence, rushing round like 15 headless chickens at the speed of light we would pose England no special problems. With nothing to do but attack, they would

51

have the opportunity of building up a record score. To sprint here, there and everywhere, like demented Keystone Cops sticking fingers furiously in the dam in the forlorn hope of stemming the flood would be a futile, negative gesture. So I made my bold decision, but I had my doubts a few minutes later when after my second penalty goal, Steve Smith scored England's fourth try to add to the two scored by Carleton and the one by Mike Slemen earlier. We were 23–6 down and I was faced with the distinct possibility that my first game as captain might well be my last.

However, the final half hour was a revelation and with a blind faith in our collective decision to go down in a blaze of glory we staged a tremendous recovery in a fantastic, exhilarating exhibition of running rugby. In particular it is worth mentioning that Jim Renwick and John Rutherford were in dazzling form and put on a superb display with their elusive, jinking running. We actually won the last quarter of the match 12–7, scoring two splendid tries and coming very close to scoring three others. In the end we lost 30–18 but as we all trooped off the pitch at the final whistle I shook Bill Beaumont's hand, congratulated him on winning the match, the Triple Crown, the Championship and the Grand Slam and saying that although we had lost and I was disappointed at the result, I had thoroughly enjoyed the match and it had been immense fun to be part of such a smashing game. People often assume it must be unbearable and embarrassingly humiliating to lose by such a score in an international but that is simply not the case.

I reckon that if our team that day had played that England side ten times, we would have lost ten times and if we had met 20 times we might just have sneaked one win with a little bit of luck. To me it was no disgrace to lose to a much better-equipped all-round side and I felt quite chuffed that by our brave, adventurous policy in the second half we had at least gone down fighting all the way in a memorable finale to England's finest hour in 20 years.

At the time and in the past five years there has been a strong move in the media to belittle British rugby to such an extent that each country which finishes the season perched in splendid isolation on the top of the table is supposed to have achieved glory only because the other four countries are so bad that it's a case of crushing the blind school four times. I accept that Ireland's success in 1982 and 1985 and Scotland's ultimate triumph in 1984 did rely to some degree on the relative weakness of European rugby in the 1980s and more than an even share of good luck. But the fact is that they finished top dogs and deserved full credit and congratulations for that effort. Furthermore I would argue most vociferously that England's Grand Slam is put in best perspective by placing it as the last outstanding achievement of the ten-year period between 1971 and 1980 which has to be seen as a golden era of British rugby. The England pack in my view was slightly superior to the respective packs of both Wales and France when they completed Grand Slam triumphs three times between them in the previous four years.

If I had picked the best set of forwards for the British Lions tests in South Africa in 1980 I would have included at least six of that England pack and possibly seven – John Scott being the exception. On the other hand, the England backs that year could not be considered in the same league as the great Welsh stars of the mid- and late seventies or even the best of the French in their championship winning sides of 1977 and 1981. Steve Smith was a clever scrum half and his shrewd tactical brain was vitally important to England. He had most of the skills of the great scrum halves but he lacked a yard of pace to break decisively and had to rely on his strength rather than his speed to breach opposition defences. This is never quite so successful at the highest level and, in consequence, England would have been even more dynamic with Gareth Edwards or Terry Holmes at scrum half and Barry John or Phil Bennett at fly half. These last two were able to do everything John Horton did and a lot more besides. England would have been delighted too if they had had players like J.P.R. Williams and Gerald Davies to add that extra dimension to their play, but even if they were not as outstanding either individually or collectively as the best of the Welsh, they worked efficiently as a unit and deserved full recognition for their part in the Grand Slam success. Paul Dodge, Mike Slemen and John Carleton were equally valuable and crucial because they could all create and score tries in attack but they were also exceptionally good defensive players. They were decisive tacklers and also excellent at sweeping up in defence and covering the full back. The strength of British rugby in the past ten years would be best exemplified by the England pack of 1980 and the Welsh backs of 1978. Having said that, I doubt that any side in Europe in the 1980s would have beaten the England Grand Slam side – the overall standard has gradually slipped in the past five years.

The following year we suffered another defeat in an equally thrilling and dramatic match. It was a lovely sunny day at Twickenham which was rewarded with endless exciting open rugby culminating in six tries and a feast of good attacking play. Clive Woodward scored a classic try jinking past half of our team for the score of a lifetime and Huw Davies, the new England fly half, won the match with an incredible try which began in deep defence with Slemen and Carleton leading the counter-attack and it ended with Davies weaving his way past a handful of Scots before sprinting clear. Davies had a most impressive first international, and apart from being a dynamic tackler he kicked well to make life quite hard for me. In many ways, I feel a full back plays half of every match against the opposition fly half whether he passes or kicks, and, contrary to the information that had been fed to us by our moles, Davies was a fine tactician, a most competent kicker and, as we already knew, a talented player.

As the 1981 match was unforgettable, so the 1982

game was eminently forgettable. It was a dull 9–9 draw and the only highlight or redeeming feature for me was the penalty which I kicked in the dying moments when Colin Smart was, perhaps harshly, penalized for jostling Ian Paxton off the ball in midfield just inside our half. It was one of the longest penalties I ever kicked and it was a satisfactory end to an unsatisfactory match.

It was a pity that my last Calcutta Cup match should be so uninspiring but the weather was dreadful with a howling gale making it impossible to play with any control. Nevertheless, the majority of games against England had been splendid adverts for the game of rugby and more often than not both sides went to great lengths to produce a spectacle worth watching. The blunt truth is that England ought to be challenging hard for the championship every year with their rich resources but their basic structure leaves the hapless selectors with a hopeless task. However, by some inspired and unbeliev-able selection they have compounded the felony by defying logic and flying in the face of reason on far too many occasions. Several times in the seventies, I heaved a huge sigh of relief when I heard the names of the England team to play us. Since 1972, they have picked a score of players whom I would never have lobbed into a lucky bag in the first place. They have made more disastrous selectorial decisions than any of the other international board countries in my experience, thereby reducing the England side to a shadow of its true potential. I know from many long conversations with the established England players that they have been just as horrified and frustrated at all sorts of banal and bizarre choices which have contributed substantially to Eng-land's moderate record with the exception of 1980. That was the one year in my memory that they really did make the best use of the talent available, and that is why that side would provide almost everyone if I had to name the best 15 English players from the ten Calcutta Cup games in which I played.

The best attacking full back England have had in that

period has been Marcus Rose who was big, strong and fast and a good footballer. Alistair Hignell has been their best defensive player in that position, but I would choose Dusty Hare because he was a mixture of both, if not as good as either in their specialist strength, and he was also an indecently reliable goal-kicker. The best two wings were Carleton and Slemen although I must point out that when I played against David Duckham he was past his days of glory and, in the twilight of his career, he had one or two shockers against us. At his best, he was devastating but I never faced him at his best. In the centre, I would pick Dodge for his tight defence, sound skills and good support play and his club colleague Clive Woodward who has been one of the most entertaining and underrated players in British rugby. After those two I would rate the very fast and elusive Coventry pair, Geoff Evans and Peter Preece, the most dangerous runners England have had, but I would just prefer Dodge and Woodward. I would complete the exact Grand Slam back division with Steve Smith and John Horton at half back. Smithy was far and away the best English scrum-half throughout my decade and it has always surprised me he was dropped from time to time – poorer players have had a lot of games for the British Lions – and he is also fantastic value off the field. In a sport which needs characters, he is in a class of his own. Alan Old was the most reliable fly half and I think Huw Davies has had the greatest potential despite being repeatedly messed about by the selectors, but I would stick with John Horton.

Up front, I would make just two changes from the Grand Slam pack. I would replace Maurice Colclough with Nigel Horton and in the back row I would switch Roger Uttley to number eight in place of John Scott, with Peter Dixon coming in on the blind-side flank. This means that top-class players like prop Mike Burton and Stack Stevens, hooker John Pullin and flanker Mike Rafter would miss out, but that all goes to emphasize how strong England were in 1980.

That composite side, which includes 13 of the Grand Slam team, would take a great deal of beating and Bill Beaumont would be the man to captain them. He has long fulfilled the typical image of the British bulldog spirit and, like the England team, I have a tremendous respect and admiration for him. He led by example, he was always totally selfless, usually beavering away at the bottom of every ruck, he was a great sportsman in every sense and yet he was a hard man. He represented everything good about English rugby and despite all the ups and downs there has been a lot to admire. The infuriating thing from an English point of view is that success is so infrequent. 1980 should happen every two or three years, and with the right system, the right selectors and the right players, it probably would happen that regularly.

4

Up Against Wales

My first match against Wales coincided with my first win for Scotland and because of this it will always have a special significance for me. It turned out to be doubly important as we beat a Welsh side which contained not only nine British Lions but several of my personal rugby heroes. In my innocent youth I had placed players like J.P.R. Williams, Gerald Davies, Phil Bennett and Gareth Edwards on a pedestal balanced precariously on the top rung of rugby's ladder. The rest of us were mere mortals, anchored at ground level, gazing skywards in awe and admiration. Yet, on 3 February 1973, the superstars tumbled down to earth with a resounding thump and I learned some poignant lessons; rugby is a funny game where reputations count for little and all men are equal in the eyes of William Webb Ellis. Wales had won the previous five games against Scotland and were generally expected to sweep us aside just as easily as they had crucified England two weeks earlier running up 25 points in the process including five tries.

The Murrayfield amphitheatre was ready for the Scottish Christians to be sacrificed to the Welsh lions, but it is strange how such a threat can be exactly the inspiration the underdog requires. I firmly believe that sheer cussed spirit, commitment and wholehearted endeavour will often help the technically inferior or less gifted side to triumph. And over the years Scotland and Ireland, more than any other countries, have produced some major surprises when least expected, by hustling better sides out of their rhythm to such an extent that they never recover in time to save the match. That crisp February afternoon was just such a day.

Ian McLauchlan was made captain for the first time although the previous incumbent, Peter Brown, retained his place in the team. The approach to captaincy from McLauchlan and Brown was totally different – almost at opposite ends of the spectrum. P.C. Brown leaned heavily towards the intellectual approach and was decidedly up market with a liberal sprinkling of choice quotations from the likes of Burns, Chaucer and Shakespeare. McLauchlan, more a man of the earth, relied on a passionate, blood-curdling appeal to man's basic instincts of aggression and survival. After a couple of seasons being jollied along by the purple passages of Henry the Fifth's call to arms at Agincourt, McLauchlan was unable to betray his tough Jordanhill background. Perhaps I was very impressionable as a tender youth in his initial introduction to the mystical ways of international rugby but I remember that particular team talk more vividly than any other that I heard throughout my career.

Life is made up of artists and artisans and McLauchlan belonged in the latter category. He was a worker and a grafter, *par excellence*, and he led and inspired by example. Like Bill Beaumont, he never asked any of his troops to undertake any task which he would not willingly do himself. He was, even by the strictest standards of Glasgow, as cited in McArthur Kingsley-Long's vividly descriptive book, *No Mean City*, a hard, hard man. He began by informing us that we were going to hear a completely different style of team talk, delivered in his own basic way, and for a start we could forget all recent team talks and could stuff Burns, Chaucer and Shakespeare into oblivion. If memory serves me right after all these years, I believe he actually used an even stronger, more emotive word than 'stuff'!

The point was well made. All too often I have heard captains go through the motions of trying to impart a vigorous pep talk but fail because they were not actually deeply, emotionally involved themselves. That can lead to embarrassing slips for the tongue like the captain who demanded 80 per cent for 100 minutes or insisted on everyone producing a thud and blunder approach; the Mighty Mouse was on a different plane. McLauchlan made it abundantly clear that day what was at stake, and in the most straightforward and pugnacious manner what he expected from each and every one of us, both the fearless and the faint-hearted. With typical forthright naked aggression he delivered his challenge in simple, sharp tones. Every word was measured and punched out with deadly intent; every sentence was loaded with dramatic rhetoric even if the occasional word was not to be found in the standard Oxford dictionary. He was a man with a mission and he was not going to be easily sidetracked. I can still feel the shiver run up my spine when I relive the mental picture of McLauchlan haranguing us with his team talk that day, and reminding us that we had to be prepared to sacrifice our bodies or risk letting him down, letting down our coach and our country.

That certainly was not my style and I'm pleased to report that I never did and never could deliberately injure anyone on a rugby pitch in the pursuit of amateur sport. But even the prima donnas in the backs got the message that we were not expected to lie down like dead ants and allow the Welsh to trample all over us as they had in the previous few matches. His whole attitude was ruthless, with the consequence that it was a fairly ruthless, brutal match.

It was not an edifying spectacle to the neutral spectator but for the committed fan it was a profoundly intriguing clash of wills. Our forwards played magnificently and, suitably locked into the McLauchlan philosophy, they seemed to strike the fear of death into a surprisingly stunned and hesitant Welsh team. Although Wales had all their famous backs on show, our simple tactical approach was to beat them up front and then mount a 60-second security guard every minute of the match on Gareth Edwards. Dougie Morgan at scrum half and Jock Millican and Nairn McEwan on the flanks vied with each other to take over the mantle of Gareth's shadow every moment the ball was in play. Not once did Edwards escape their clutches, and with our pack on top and our backs tackling anything and everything in red that moved, it was a fabulous feeling of overwhelming satisfaction at the end when we won by the convincing margin of two tries to nil.

We scored our points in the first 20 minutes with tries from Colin Telfer and Billy Steele and one conversion by Dougie Morgan. Phil Bennett and John Taylor managed three penalties between them for Wales but we were more emphatic winners than the margin of one point would suggest. It was a pleasant sensation to have a plan of action, to follow it through relentlessly and to see it prevail. It was great to be in a winning Scottish side at my third attempt and especially reassuring to overcome such a star-studded Welsh side. This psychological injection of confidence meant that I was never overawed when playing against sides in the Five Nations Championship during the rest of my career.

The following year in Cardiff, Wales were much better prepared and they just about deserved their win in a tight game which involved another dimension since the British Lions party to tour South Africa was due to be announced at the end of the season. The only try of the match was created by the unique wizardry of Gerald Davies and, unfortunately, I was on the receiving end of one of his famous lightning side-steps. He had the unusual knack of accelerating into and out of a jink when most mortals have to slow down and he was incredibly hard to stop if he had any room at all in which to manoeuvre. He did in that game, midway through the first half from a heel against the head which caught us flat-footed and, after sliding past the initial despairing defenders, he was pinging down the right wing with myself and Colin Telfer covering across to head him off. I do not know who invented the phrase 'now you see him, now you don't' but Telfer and I realized the meaning of it as we groped thin air while Davies jack-knifed off his right foot at blistering speed inside both of us to set up a try for Terry Cobner. It was the sort of aesthetic, athletic brilliance which deserves to win matches.

In 1975, Wales won the championship with crushing victories over France in Paris and England at Cardiff, before they played us, and then over Ireland in the last game of the season. They scored an amazing 77 points in those three wins, including 13 tries, and it was extremely gratifying for the Scots to come between Wales and a Grand Slam at Murrayfield in front of a world record crowd for a rugby union international.

In those days the capacity of Murrayfield was 80,000 but it was not an all-ticket match and it seemed that the whole of Wales had travelled north in expectation of a high-scoring victory. The whole of Edinburgh was a sea of red and white scarves from the Monday through to the Saturday and it was estimated that as many as 40,000 Welsh supporters were in town. The tactics those supporters adopt are the same every time. One guy books the hotel room and three of his friends join him with sleeping bags on the floor each night. Come Saturday, the majority still have not fallen over a ticket for the game and they happily dive into a glass of Tartan bitter and watch the match live on television in Edinburgh. Suitably hung over, they crawl into their minibus the next day and, piled high to the roof, they set off on the return journey.

In 1975 most of them managed to find their way into the ground, although not all that many succeeded in seeing the game. 104,000 were jam-packed inside the perimeter fence of the stadium but 20,000 of those could see nothing of the game. The Scottish team arrived an hour and a quarter before the kick-off and we went straight out to see the state of the pitch and the strength of the wind and generally soak up the atmosphere in our build-up. That day was unique. The terraces were crammed to the gunnels in a remarkable scenario resembling blue-and-white and red-and-white sardines squeezed together into a giant tin, guaranteeing themselves a place in the *Guinness Book of Records*. Apparently, the roads from the centre of town to the ground were packed for over two hours beforehand, and when the gates were eventually locked with 104,000 inside, it was estimated that another 25,000 were listening to the commentary outside on BBC Radio.

Wales scored the only try with, would you believe, another scintillating break and series of side steps from Gerald Davies which led to Trevor Evans crossing over in the corner in the last minute of proper time. The conversion from Allan Martin narrowly failed and three penalties by Dougie Morgan and a drop goal by Ian McGeechan was sufficient to give us our last victory over Wales until 1981.

The next year in Cardiff, Wales extracted full revenge and I reckon their side that year was the best of the nine I played against without a single weak link in it. They were an incredibly strong team, as can be gauged from the fact that every one of their side that day had been picked for at least one British Lions tour. The famous Pontypool front row ruled British scrums in that period, they had three big line-out men in Allan Martin, Geoff Wheel and Mervyn Davies to give them plenty of options, and their loose forwards, Mervyn, Terry Cobner and Trevor Evans were all fast, skilful footballers. Chuck in behind that sort of pack Bennett and Edwards at half-back, and then, even if you included five players illiterate in the basic grammar of the game you would still be guaranteed a reasonably successful season. As it happened though, the five who did in fact make up the numbers would have been good enough to perform miracles behind a beaten pack and a modest pair of half-backs. They had two potential match-winners on the wings in Gerald Davies and J.J. Williams and the man for all seasons, J.P.R. Williams, at full back. He was the best defensive full back in the world in the 1970s and he could make a useful dent in the opposition when he adopted the role of running full back in attack. Steve Fenwick was the steady midfield player who seemed to spark off the attacks and Ray Gravell, the other centre, was a powerful, strong runner who added a turbo-charged thrust to complement the more elusive skills of those around him. The relative strength of Wales that day was best exemplified by the fact that only two of the Scottish side – Gordon Brown and, possibly, Ian McLauchlan – would have been good enough to force their way into the Welsh XV.

The only moment I enjoyed was scoring a try after a sweeping attack down the left flank which I rounded off. However, that was our only score and the rest of the game belonged largely to a great Welsh side who went on to win the Grand Slam. Gareth Edwards scored a superb individual try, selling a couple of dummies and accelerating from the 25-yard line through our defence to cap a superb performance. Phil Bennett converted this try to earn himself a special place in the statistical record books with his 92nd point for Wales, thereby passing Barry John's previous record total of 90. The other reason people still talk about the 1976 game concerns the referee, Dr Cuny. He pulled a leg muscle very badly early in the second half but he refused to allow one of the touch-judges to take over the control of the match. Instead, rather pathetically, he limped along often 40 or 50 yards behind play, missing all sorts of offences in the process. As someone pointed out afterwards, if he'd have been a horse or a dog he would have been put down to save him from further suffering. Without doubt it made a mockery of the match but there is no question that the better side won and it might have been 40–6 not 28–6 if Wales had had a dash more luck.

In the last five years of the seventies, Wales and France were so dominant and had so many good players that the championship was more or less divided into a first division for those two teams and a second division for the rest of us. We lost the next four matches against Wales and only the 1977 game is worth mentioning in any detail. In their 18–9 win at Murrayfield we managed to score one good try which was some consolation for a poor season. Dougie Morgan broke from a scrum and put Jim Renwick through a half-gap. I charged into the line from full back, took the ball from Renwick on the burst and accelerated clear of J. P. R. Williams and the cover defence to score. I thought it was a fairly decent effort but it was nothing compared to the try scored at the end of the game by Phil Bennett. I had a hand in that score, too, because my speculative kick ahead was caught by J. P. R. Williams who ran out of defence before the ball was passed along to Gerald Davies. He jinked inside and outside the initial handful of would-be tacklers, linked with Burcher and Edwards who found Bennett up on the outside to continue the attack from half way. Bennett mesmerized a few more defenders, myself included, leaving a trail of navy blue jerseys floundering on the ground in his wake. He touched down between the posts for the most spectacular try of the championship and probably the best of the decade.

I dropped out of the 1978 match through injury – the only international I missed between winning my first cap and my 51st cap. In 1979 John Rutherford won his first cap for Scotland and my lasting memory of that game was John coming up to me after a line-out in only the second minute to ask my advice, because the Welsh flanker, Paul Ringer, had just told him that if he touched the ball once more in the whole game he guaranteed he would break his neck. As a seasoned veteran, I told 'Rud' not to worry and pointed out that Ringer was guilty of just a pitiful piece of gamesmanship. On the other hand, I added, unless he had excellent medical insurance I would not advise him going for too many inside breaks.

Ringer was not the sort of player I would ever want in my team but fortunately 'Rud' was easily able to cope with him, and in the first half he got his confidence when he sliced through a gap to make an overlap. After two or three quick passes, Alan Tomes floated a long, high ball up to the wing, and having raced up from full back I was there to catch the ball and step inside the cover to score a try. I more or less scored again in 1981 when we beat Wales 15–6 because in a tense kick and chase to the line, Gareth Davies, realizing I was going to beat him, was desperate enough to grab my jersey and pull me back in open play around the Welsh 25-yard line with no one else near us. I still managed to keep marginally in front of him but, as I was about to dive on the ball over the line, he obstructed me again and further interfered with me. The referee, David Burnett, had no hesitation in awarding Scotland a penalty try which clinched the match for us. The Welsh played badly that day and two of their long-serving backs, J. P. R. Williams and Steve Fenwick, were dropped for the Irish match two weeks later, never to be picked for Wales again. It was a sad end, especially for J. P. R., who was made to look unusually ordinary by the dreadful, windy conditions and by the splendid tactical kicking of John Rutherford. He was labouring to chase the rolling, diagonal kick, and it was obvious to everyone that his best days were behind him.

He had actually retired at the end of the 1979 season, but like so many sportsmen who make a comeback after years at the top, he wished afterwards that he had not. Muhammad Ali made exactly the same mistake in 1980 and, like Ali, J. P. R. was a shadow of his former greatness. It was a shame that one of rugby's legends should end his international career dropped in ignominy. His reputation was soon to suffer further damage when he became involved in a court case against John Reason and the *Daily Telegraph*. Williams had written his autobiography and took legal action against the *Telegraph* for suggesting he had professionalized himself by taking money out of the game. The judge directed the jury in his favour but three Court of Appeal judges found unanimously that the original judge had misdirected the jury. They ordered a re-trial, but J. P. R. decided to drop the case. People have been highly critical of J. P. R. in the past four years but I can only speak as I find.

I found him a fairly intense individual who was not

only physically, but also mentally, tough. By any standards he was a magnificent world-class player in his prime, and I know that from 1972 until he first retired in 1979 there is absolutely no doubt that if I had had to select a combined Scotland-Wales side, I would always have put J. P. R. ahead of myself. 1981 is a different story but in the seventies he was in a class of his own. Off the field we got on pretty well, and he was always friendly. Considering he was super confident of his own ability, he tended to be reasonably humble in defeat. None the less, I enjoyed playing against him, as it was always an extra special challenge. I knew I was faster and more elusive than he was, and I always relished those occasional head-to-head confrontations when I had the ball and was able to take him on. Admittedly, when it came to fielding the high ball with the All Blacks pack in close proximity with their studs rattling on the ground, or crash-tackling locks backwards, or falling on the ball just as the French forwards arrived, there has never been a player to compare with J. P. R. Williams.

I should imagine that he was quite glad that he was not playing full back for Wales in 1982 against us in Cardiff. That match, which was to be my last against Wales and my last international in Europe, was one of the half a dozen special matches I will always look back on with particular pride. We had not won a match in Cardiff since 1962 but at least when our number did come up we did it in style. I had spent my life dreaming of thumping Wales in Cardiff and the All Blacks at Murrayfield. However, by 1982, after ten years of trying in vain, I was resigned to the fact that such heroic wins were likely to remain the stuff of dreams. I wanted to beat Wales, just once, by 20 or 30 points in front of their own supporters, although I was intrigued to hear a great Scottish lock forward of my vintage who had been on the receiving end of one or two traumatic reversals at the hands of the Welsh, put forward a quite different view point. In his ultimate dream, he confided, Scotland, the rabid underdogs, would beat Wales at Cardiff 4–3 in the fifth minute of injury time with a bitterly disputed, highly controversial try, which the slow-motion replay on television would prove conclusively afterwards was not a try at all. These degrading emotions were inspired, if that is the right word, by the fact that 20 years of drought is a long time for rugby players thirsty for victory.

Funnily enough, as captain of Scotland on 15 occasions, I had always wanted to play good rugby and use our backs, but it would not be true to claim that the coach, Jim Telfer, and myself had made elaborate plans to throw the ball around willy-nilly as many pundits supposed afterwards.

My whole game was based on running at and attacking the opposition but when our proven pack of the mid and late seventies broke up, we had to forage and destroy in the manner of Ireland and then make the best use of the scraps of possession which did come our way. In pre-match planning, it would have been foolhardy and optimistic to anticipate the dramatic decline in Wales that afternoon. Dressed in red, all they needed to complete the Santa Claus image was long white beards, because they gave us so many presents it would have been difficult for us not to win. None the less, our plan was to tear into our tackles and generally try to upset the rhythm of the opposition and hustle them into making mistakes. When we won the ball we intended to take them on with our fast, nippy backs like David Johnston, Jim Renwick and Roger Baird who might be expected to wrong-foot bigger, less agile players like Bob Ackerman and Ray Gravell. Since France won at Cardiff in 1968, Wales had survived 27 matches in the Five Nations Championship unbeaten. We had prepared for a rough, tough match and the last thing I imagined would happen was a runaway victory with a try count of 5–1 in our favour. We had scored nine tries altogether in the previous 40 years in our 15 matches at Cardiff Arms Park, so scoring seven tries in 1982 and 1984 showed how much progress we had made recently or demonstrated just how far Wales had regressed. It is an interesting statistic that in the 1980s Ireland twice, England and Scotland have all captured the Triple Crown, but Wales last achieved such an honour in 1979.

Gareth Davies, who had been the hero for Wales on other days, was the unwitting villain this time. He was largely responsible for what is popularly known nowadays as the ten-point try. Wales, already three-nil up, were on the attack deep inside our half with a two-man overlap and looking sure to score when, unaccountably, Gareth Davies squandered a golden opportunity, by kicking the ball ahead. Instead of scoring a try, Wales suddenly found themselves on the retreat and in desperate disarray. Roger Baird collected the ball near the touch-line and bravely launched a counter-attack. Iain Paxton and Alan Tomes were up in support to continue the attack and finally Jim Calder careered over the line to score the try of the season in a sensational move covering almost the whole length of the pitch. It was a magnificent spectacle and it meant that instead of trailing seven or nine points to nil, we were actually in the lead.

Wales then seemed to panic and Gareth Davies ran the ball more than we expected which played right into our hands. In two midfield disasters, Gravell was knocked over by Calder deep in our half and Jim Renwick sprinted the length of the field to score, and then Wales made a mess of another attempt to run the ball which allowed David Johnston to hack it through for Jim Pollock to score in the corner. Derek White and David Johnston completed the try count and I managed four conversions to give us a final winning margin of 34–18.

On a day of records, we inflicted on the Welsh the highest total ever scored against them by any country in Wales. It was a tremendous victory although, in fairness, part of the reason for the high score was the ineptitude of the Welsh. Their tactical approach was all wrong, and Gareth Davies had his worst game for Wales on one of those dreadful days when absolutely nothing goes right. It is quite possible that he was not fully fit, but he had such a nightmare that he disappeared from all Welsh teams for three years, sunk without trace.

The demise of Davies would not happen so readily in other countries where ready-made reserves are not queuing up to step in at a moment's notice, but Wales have a well-known assembly line which specializes in manufacturing brilliant fly halves. It is important to appreciate that rugby is the national sport in Wales in precisely the same way that it is in New Zealand and South Africa. That is why from a relatively small population they do exceptionally well and why rugby means so much to the entire country. It is a sobering thought that they have now gone six seasons without winning the Five Nations Championship. Such a long losing sequence has only occurred on one other occasion in the past 50-odd years. They have such a single-minded determination and pride, and the club structure is basically so sound, that you can be sure they will bounce back in the next couple of years or British rugby will be the worse for it. It will not do them any harm to have had this recent nadir in their fortunes and to have had to come to terms with the sort of problems other countries experience year in and year out.

The stark truth is that they hit the jackpot in the 1970s beyond their wildest imagination, and they had so many world-class players that if two or three of them had an off day, the others would do the honours. They had enough potential match-winners to make it positively dangerous to try and mark one or two of them out of the game since this would give all the more opportunity to different, equally indecently talented, stars. I would have loved to have played with a back division containing such gifted individuals on a regular basis, but at least I am grateful that I sampled the flavour in 1974 on the British Lions tour.

Life may have turned sour in the last five seasons for Wales but because rugby is the sport of the working class, the middle class and indeed every class there, it is only a matter of time before they rule the roost again. Nevertheless, hardly any of the current side would find a place in the best 15 Welsh players I have played against between 1972 and 1982. J.P.R. would be full back, with Gerald Davies and J.J. Williams on the wings. Steve Fenwick and Ray Gravell were the best pair of centres and Bennett and Edwards were the best half-backs. People often tell me that Bennett was not a good fly half for getting a three-quarter line moving and he must have been terrible for a full back trying to time his run into the line because he often drifted across field, but I can state categorically that I found him superb to play with and, with the possible exception of John Rutherford, Phil has been my favourite fly half in the last ten years. He liked to run and he liked to bring the full back in as the extra man and I found it incredibly easy to play with him. No other fly half has used me so generously and I look back on all our games together with real pleasure.

I doubt that the Welsh pack were ever quite as formidable as either the French or English Grand Slam forwards, but they still had some uncommonly useful players. Put Allan Martin and Geoff Wheel behind the Pontypool front row with Mervyn Davies at number 8 and Terry Cobner and Trevor Evans on the flank and the backs were unlikely to have to survive on starvation rations. To their credit Wales usually tried to use those backs and play an expansive brand of rugby. As a result the Scotland–Wales matches were usually exciting and entertaining, always hard and uncompromising and generally very rewarding. Suffice to conclude they were very special internationals and a win over Wales was something to be treasured for ever and a day.

5

The Passion and Pride of Ireland

Unlike the majority of the internationals I played against
England and Wales, which were usually entertaining
and enjoyable matches, my ten games against Ireland
were less flamboyant and spectacular encounters. One
important reason for this contrast was the bad weather
which ruined over half of the Irish matches before the
kick-off. It is all very well for the rugby correspondents of
the various newspapers to criticize two teams for producing a dull afternoon's entertainment, but on a sodden
pitch, in driving rain with a greasy, slippery ball and a
howling wind to be negotiated it is not easy to play
attractive rugby. In no match is that more true than
against the Irish. They feed like predators on every
mistake the opposition make and on a filthy day they are
in their element. Conditions were very rarely kind to us
when we played Ireland but if few of the ten games were
riveting at least there were plenty of memorable
moments.

Without being hypercritical, it is also worth pointing
out that of all the sides in the Five Nations Championship, Ireland have played the least ambitious and
enterprising rugby in recent years. They stick fairly
rigidly to a destructive, negative approach to ensure
making the best use of their limited resources, and in
fairness to them they are an extremely difficult side to
dominate. They have tremendous commitment and
spirit and often perform minor miracles in beating much

more fancied teams. Scotland have always respected their intense will to win and I think we have usually been better prepared than some of the other countries who seem to have fallen into the trap of becoming over-complacent because, on paper, Ireland look relatively weak. I know that the Irish have always been dangerous opponents with a handful of outstanding players in each of their sides and the rest prepared to fight till they drop.

Although the technical quality of many Scotland–Ireland matches was perhaps not in the same league as the France–Wales games of the 1970s, the endeavour and enthusiasm is unrivalled and I am relieved to recount that in beating them five times and drawing once, Ireland were the only side in the Championship against whom I finished winning more games than I lost. It all began promisingly in 1973 when, after five Irish victories in succession since 1967, we struck the winning trail again in what was probably the most exciting, interesting and controversial game of the series. Ireland scored two tries to one but I still felt we deserved to win; we lost Ian McLauchlan with a broken leg shortly before half-time which partially disrupted our fluency and also I was convinced one of the Irish tries should not have been allowed. We trailed 10–9 at half-time after Dougie Morgan had kicked two penalties and dropped a goal for us and Barry McGann had landed two penalties for Ireland and had created a neat try down the blind side from a scrum for Wallace McMaster.

Ian McGeechan dropped a goal to give us the lead momentarily, but then Tom Kiernan, in his fifty-fourth and final appearance for Ireland, was awarded a try. This followed a move started by Mike Gibson and continued by McMaster. He passed to Kiernan, up on his outside with myself the only obstacle between him and the try-line. I tackled the Irish captain just short of the line and we both crashed in a heap into touch, the corner flag and touch-in goal as Kiernan grounded the ball. I felt at the time the referee had the choice of giving us a line-out on our own line when I forced Tom into

73

touch just before he grounded the ball or a 25-yard drop-out as both of us were swept into touch in goal via the corner flag. To my surprise he awarded a try, but, thankfully, it did not affect the result and such a wonderful moment could not possibly have happened to a nicer, more popular and more deserving player than Tom Kiernan. To score a try in his final match was a great end to a great career and no-one, certainly not me, could possibly begrudge him it.

Just what a wonderful sportsman he was emerged shortly afterwards near the very end of the game. Kiernan's try made it 14–12 to Ireland, but in the dying minutes I joined the three-quarter line at full speed, side-stepped inside the cover defence to link with that well-known running lock forward Alastair McHarg, who gave the crucial scoring pass to Ian Forsyth. McHarg was the most unconventional player I ever came across and he was once marvellously described by a journalist who wrote that inside the big 6 foot 5 inch frame of the Scottish second-row forward, there was an inside centre or a fly half trying to get out. McHarg used to appear from nowhere as if through a trapdoor in the ground, but never was it more important than for that try which regained the lead for us that day at Murrayfield. Ireland redoubled their efforts but with time running rapidly out one of their last-ditch attacks came to grief, we broke into their half and Morgan attempted to drop his third goal of the match. It seemed to fall just short under the bar and only one man knew for sure whether it was over or not. That man was Tom Kiernan who was right under the crossbar running back as the ball dipped down. The referee was too far behind play to know for sure and so were the rest of the players. If Kiernan had touched the ball down there was a possibility that Ireland would have been awarded a 25-yard drop-out and they could have had one more fling at getting the three points they needed to win.

However, Kiernan threw one arm up in the air to signal to the referee and the capacity crowd that the ball was over. It was a magnanimous gesture of goodwill, an act of true sportsmanship that I will always treasure because it summed up everything that is good in rugby. It was a generous act of a generous man and I remember thinking when the final whistle went that I was glad not just that we had won but also that Tom Kiernan had scored his try early in the second half. I think I could name one or two famous international full backs who might not have reacted in quite the same way to Morgan's drop goal, but in my opinion they would be poorer people for it and would have difficulty in living with their own consciences.

The only comparable incident I can recall was when, in equally doubtful circumstances, Barry John had a drop at goal for Wales against Ireland a few years previously. It appeared to most people present to have narrowly failed, but amidst all the general uncertainty Mike Gibson, the nearest man to the posts, raised an arm high in the air to sportingly signal to everyone the three points for Wales. The nearest parallel would be in cricket when a fielder attempts a diving catch and only he knows if he caught the ball immediately before it could touch the ground. If Kiernan or Gibson happened to be the fielder and claimed a fair catch and I was the batsman, then I would walk back to the pavilion happy in the knowledge that I had been fairly dismissed. I like to think that in similar circumstances I, and the majority of rugby players, would have reacted in exactly the same way as Kiernan and Gibson. There is no way such a philanthropic philosophy would be shared by most soccer players or supporters. Indeed, it would not necessarily be the natural, instinctive reaction of professional sportsmen. I am glad that John McEnroe was not full back for Ireland in 1973.

The following year Ireland scored the only try of a disappointing match to win 9–6 but we might still have won. I kicked both our penalties in the second half but missed two others which were within my range. We won at home in 1975 but much more significant was our victory in Dublin in 1976. This was my first away win for Scotland in my twentieth international and it was a great occasion even though the game was played in appalling conditions. Not a try was scored by either side and our 15–6 win came from seven kicks at goal. I managed four penalties in eight attempts and Ron Wilson dropped a goal. For Ireland Barry McGann kicked two penalties from six attempts. In my first three seasons we had won every home match in the Championship, but had lost every away game, which meant we were left stranded in the middle of the table each season. This away win was therefore important in breaking through a psychological barrier, but it was wasted that particular year as we had lost one of our two home matches to France. An away win in any of the three preceding years would have given us at least a share of the Championship. Our pack performed especially well in the wet that day with David Leslie quite outstanding. I felt that that was very nearly the best Scottish pack of the 1970s, and in their two games together we beat England and Ireland in the last two matches of the season. McLauchlan and Carmichael were the props, Gordon Brown and Alan Tomes were the locks, with Alastair McHarg at number eight and David Leslie and Mike Biggar on the flanks.

It was a pity that after the selectors had finally got our pack right they were unable to select half of them at the start of the next season. Gordon Brown, though little did we know it at the time, played his last game for Scotland in that 1976 victory against Ireland. Injuries prevented Mike Biggar and David Leslie from playing in January 1977, and Ian McLauchlan was dropped. Our poor results that year reflected the changes in personnel in the pack. Our only win was against Ireland on yet another shocking day following persistent heavy rain. We managed to score three tries but despite the close result, 21–18, it was not a very good match.

There was a highly controversial ending to the 1978 game in Dublin when we had the opportunity to grab a draw in the final minute of injury time, but opted to run an eminently kickable penalty instead. We trailed 12–9 when Ireland were penalized at a line-out ten yards from their own line and Dougie Morgan, in his first match as captain, would have had little difficulty in landing his fourth penalty of the afternoon. In principle, I am a firm believer in trying flat out to win; if you cannot achieve that target, then to try and force a draw is next best. But in the special circumstances on that particular day I fully supported and applauded Dougie Morgan's decision to take a tapped penalty and try to score a try to win the game. We ran the ball but the Irish defence tackled like tigers to snuff out the move and then the final whistle went. Ireland could scarcely believe their luck and, not surprisingly, there was concerted criticism heaped on Morgan afterwards for not kicking the relatively simple goal and beginning the season in decent style with an away draw.

My argument, and I dare say Morgan's argument, is that there were very good motives for trying to win rather than draw even if the odds were stacked against us. The critics rightly pointed out that we had failed to score a try in the preceding 95 minutes of a match involving 15 minutes of injury time, and argued that we were most unlikely to score one at a time when the Irish defence, seconds away from victory, was going to be at its tightest. But what people should remember is that this was the first match of the Championship that season and Scotland had not won the Triple Crown for exactly 40 years. Every year since 1938, the Scots had set out full of hope that history would be repeated. It is said that absence makes the heart grow fonder and with each passing year we increased our efforts to chase the glory that last courted us before the Second World War. If we had drawn with Ireland in January 1978, as we could so easily have done, that would have automatically meant our dreams of the Triple Crown dashed for another 12 months. Had it been the last match of the season with nothing at stake or the opening match against France, then, of course, we should have settled for the draw, but if people accept that every year for 11 years I began each new season with hopes and ambitions to win the Triple Crown, then perhaps they will find it easier to understand why I subscribed to the tiny minority who fully approved of Morgan's controversial decision. We snatched defeat from the jaws of a draw but had I been captain I would have made the same choice.

Ironically enough, the next year we did draw at Murrayfield in a game ruined by a gale force wind. The wind and the rain again spoiled the spectacle at Lansdowne Road in 1980 when Ireland won convincingly. My last victory for Scotland against Ireland, in 1981, was played in a torrential downpour throughout and I can recall only two incidents of any note. In the first half Bruce Hay intercepted the ball during an Irish attack near the Scottish 25 and he had to run 75 yards to score. Bruce was not, for all his many talents, a sprinter, but fortunately the only Irishman in a position to give chase was Tony Ward, another extremely skilful footballer, but no speed merchant. Jim Renwick commented that it was the only time he had seen a try scored in slow motion except on TV! The only other try in the match was made by me. I fell on the ball near my own line and made a break out of defence. If I had then opened out we would have had a very good chance of scoring and that sort of dramatic counter-attack, even with a dripping wet ball on a soaking pitch, was my natural inclination. For once, hanging on to a seven-point lead, I opted to err on the side of caution. I decided to play safe, only to see my attempted clearance to touch charged down by David Irwin who followed through to score a try which Ollie Campbell converted. It was a great relief to me that we finished the game clinging on to a one point victory.

My final appearance against Ireland in 1982 was played in a hurricane, and even though we scored the only try of the match, Ollie Campbell booted Ireland to victory and their third Triple Crown this century – their first since 1949 – with six penalties and one drop goal, scoring all his side's points. Although I converted a superb try by John Rutherford I proceeded to miss four penalties in succession which might have won us the match. As captain, I gave the next two kicks to Jim Renwick who succeeded with both, but by then it was too late and we were left to help Ireland celebrate their Triple Crown into the early hours of the next morning.

Funnily enough, they were able to reciprocate two years later when I sat on the bench as we eventually struck gold and laid claim to the Triple Crown. The most pleasing thing about capturing the coveted, mythical Crown was simply the fact that we had won it after a gap of 46 years, but having said that to clinch it by scoring five tries to one and inflicting our biggest ever win against Ireland in 94 matches, 32–9, made the moment of triumph all that sweeter.

I think it is important to put the triumphs of Scotland and Ireland in 1982 and 1984 into context. Wales had collected 16 Triple Crowns and England 15 up to 1984. Since the war, Scotland had failed to turn up trumps on a single occasion, and Ireland's only successes before 1982 had come in 1948 and 1949. In over 40 years from 1938 England and Wales had won 13 Triple Crowns between them, Ireland and Scotland just two. When two countries with very limited playing resources like Scotland and Ireland do succeed as they did in 1982 and 1984, it is immensely gratifying and an astounding accomplishment. The leading players will have spent hundreds and hundreds of hours training two or three nights every week for years with their clubs and will, more often than not, have flogged away on their own on one or two other occasions each week to reach peak fitness and sharpen up all their basic skills. Countless squad sessions will have been endured honing the collective talents of the international team before passing the supreme test. I must say that when the media outside the particular country in question joined forces to belittle the crowning achievements of Scotland and Ireland, I found it bitterly disappointing and in very poor taste. I have never set my faith in the paparazzi too high but I was astounded to read in some so-called quality newspapers just how desperately bad the Irish team of 1982 and the Scottish team of 1984 were supposed to be in their moment of triumph.

I would accept that the French, Welsh and English Grand Slam sides of 1977, 1978 and 1980 were better than either of those recent Scottish and Irish teams, but to blandly criticize and rip those two teams apart, pleading the total demise of British rugby in the process, is to ignore the skills, spirit and dedication of 30 sportsmen and is an insult to the people involved which does the game no service at all. For people to write, as they did, that Scotland and Ireland won simply because the other countries were worse than moderate and the whole Championship had regressed to alarming depths in the 1980s is to oversimplify a complex issue. It is only a small part of the truth. Ireland in 1982 and Scotland in 1984 were each the best side that year and the most deserving recipient of the Triple Crown and it was callous and hurtful to find sizeable chunks of the rugby press in England and Wales opting to minimize, trivialize and decry the enormity of the achievement. I would have loved one of the Fleet Street hacks to come into our dressing room straight after our victory in Dublin in 1984 and tell us that what we had done that season was worthless and meaningless in the grand scheme of life because we were, at very best, a very moderate side and the other three countries were even worse – apart from the fact that we had had outrageous luck against England because Hare had missed umpteen kicks at goal and the referee had given us victory over Wales by ignoring forward passes which led to vital scores. I would like to think that the scene in our changing room would have added a different and significant dimension. It would have told the story of a small rugby-playing country filled with passion and enthusiasm eventually fulfilling its final dream.

The media have a job to report the facts but, hopefully, they should also have a certain feeling for the game and enter into the spirit of it. After all, it is true, but not very clever, to say that John McEnroe and Martina Navratilova only win Wimbledon every year because there are simply no other better tennis players around. Similar sentiments can be aimed at Tom Watson or Severiano Ballesteros in golf or Larry Holmes in boxing or Torvill and Dean in ice dancing or Viv Richards in cricket. If someone wins the British Open Golf Championship with four rounds of 85, he still deserves the credit because he proved himself the best golfer over four days. I think Scotland and Ireland deserved equally generous treatment. When all is said and done, Scotland finished off 1984 with a Grand Slam having scored ten tries. France, second in the Championship, scored nine tries, followed by Wales in third place with five, England fourth with two tries and Ireland bottom with just one. That in itself helps to justify Scotland's place on the top of the tree and no amount of critical nit-picking will alter those facts.

In the period that I was playing international rugby, Ireland won the Championship twice, in 1974 and 1982, and both those successes were well deserved. The basic ingredients of those triumphs were fairly similar – an outstanding captain (Willie John McBride in 1974 and Ciaran Fitzgerald in 1982), a good, constructive back-row with a real flier (Fergus Slattery on both occasions), a solid scrummage with unlimited fervour and aggression from the forwards, coupled with phenomenal team spirit and a desperate will to win. Like Scotland, they had learned to make a little talent go a long way. Although they have always managed to produce a handful of world-class players each season, the rest of the team invariably compensate for what they lack in skill, with sheer undiluted enthusiasm, commitment and determination. In my experience no country can match the ferocious intensity of an Irish pack in the opening 20 minutes of an international. They may not always be the most attractive team to watch, but you have to admire and respect their single-minded dedication.

81

The inspirational qualities of McBride and Fitzgerald as outstanding Irish captains should not be underrated, nor should their contrasting fortunes as captains of the British Lions, in 1974 and 1983 respectively, lead to the conclusion that McBride was the better captain. I was not at all surprised that Fitzgerald was a relative failure in New Zealand in 1983 because I did not think he had the right personality to successfully integrate the four different nations into one team.

McBride had the necessary stature in the game and the respect of all his players to lead the Lions to their best ever tour in 1974, and he won the admiration of his team for a variety of reasons. Fitzgerald suffered a grossly unfair hammering from certain sections of the press in 1983, but nevertheless I felt he was quite the wrong man for the job. It has struck me that the criterion for picking the Lions captain seems to place too much emphasis on the outcome of the Championship in a Lions year. In 1968 Ireland finished best of the British sides, and Tom Kiernan captained the Lions. Similarly, John Dawes was appointed in 1971 after Wales had won the Championship, McBride in 1974 after Ireland topped the table, Phil Bennett in 1977 following Wales's Triple Crown, Bill Beaumont in 1980 the year of England's Grand Slam and Fitzgerald in 1983. On that basis, if there had been a Lions tour in 1984, Jim Aitken would have automatically been captain, which would have been a mistake since it is very doubtful that he could have commanded a place in the Test team on playing ability. He was a tremendous captain of Scotland but that is as far as it went, and he was not the best loose-head prop in the four home unions. Fitzgerald was in exactly the same boat and he was never in my book as good a player as Colin Deans or indeed Peter Wheeler of England. In 1977, for all that he was one of the greatest fly halves in post-war rugby and one of the most charming people you could ever hope to meet, Phil Bennett was not necessarily the right choice to captain the Lions in New Zealand. Players like Bennett, Fitzgerald and Aitken were each quite outstanding, inspirational leaders of their own country, but not the commanding figures required to lead the Lions. Willie John McBride was and Bill Beaumont was, but the presence and charisma which these two men both had is a rare gift.

McBride in 1974 captained Ireland to the title with just two wins and one draw and I think that Fitzgerald's Triple Crown and Championship in 1982 and share of the Championship in 1983 was a more impressive and significant land-mark. In my view, judged purely as captain of Ireland and forgetting all about his manifold problems with the Lions, Ciaran Fitzgerald would rank in the very top drawer, every bit as impressive and influential as Bill Beaumont was to England, Ian McLauchlan was to Scotland, Phil Bennett was to Wales, Jean-Pierre Rives was to France and Graham Mourie was to New Zealand. His detractors should recognize this, and for what he has done as captain of Ireland they should place him on the same pedestal as the other five great captains listed above. It would be churlish and petty-minded to do anything less because his failure with a very moderate Lions side should in no way detract from his incredible success with Ireland. Leading Ireland to their second Triple Crown and third Championship in four seasons in 1985 confirmed his status and was further proof, if proof were necessary, of his leadership abilities in his own environment. I would also like to mention that in contrast to their rather negative playing style during my matches against them, the manner of their performance in 1985 was spectacularly refreshing. It was their turn to be the team to play all the good rugby, and they attacked with a running and handling game which I thought would be completely beyond them. I was delighted to be proved wrong and give full credit to the enlightened and enterprising approach of their new coach, Mick Doyle, and the players.

Having made it clear that I am a great admirer of Ciaran Fitzgerald and am delighted that his talents are now being recognized outside Ireland, I would not actually include him in my best Irish side since 1972. On sheer all round ability as a hooker I would place Pat Whelan ahead of him, leaving Ciaran and Ken Kennedy to battle it out for the place on the substitute's bench. The best two props would be Ray McLoughlin and Sean Lynch with Phil Orr and Mick Fitzpatrick not all that far behind. The locks would be Willie John McBride at the front with Donal Lenihan in the middle. The back row of the early 1980s was a superb blend and with the influence of the loose forwards in modern international rugby now greater than ever before, Fergus Slattery, Willie Duggan and John O'Driscoll would be a mighty useful triumvirate. Slattery was a truly great forward, and his speed around the field was breathtaking. A tremendous support player and tireless coverer, he was strong, abrasive and ruthlessly destructive. Strangely enough, in my opinion, he was the opposite of Phil Bennett, Ciaran Fitzgerald and Jim Aitken. He was a relatively unsuccessful captain of Ireland who would have been an ideal captain of the British Lions in 1977, if he had made himself available for selection. If Willie Duggan had ever been half as fit as Slattery he would have been unstoppable. A useful auxiliary line-out player as a tail-gunner because he timed his jumping so well, he was one of the most courageous forwards I ever played with or against. In New Zealand in 1977 I shared a hotel room with him several times during the tour and his back was always an horrendous mess of stud marks. It usually resembled one of those puzzles for kids in which they have to join the forty black dots to finish up with a picture of something. The black dots on Willie's back were made by the trampling of boots as he lay on the ground protecting the ball in a dangerous situation.

The best half-backs would inevitably initiate a months' debate in Ireland but I would unhesitatingly select Colin Patterson and Ollie Campbell. John Robbie and Tony Ward would not be all that far behind but, at their best, Patterson and Campbell were two exceptionally gifted and natural players. Campbell had a sound tactical approach, a magnificent defence, an incisive break and a deadly accurate kick. He was good at unleashing a back division too, although I would like to say that I always found Ward equally easy to play with. He was often criticized by people who accused him of being too much of an individual but I found him very easy to read when we played in the same team and he was excellent in using an attacking full back at the right time and in the right way.

The best two wings over the years have been Tom Grace and Trevor Ringland with Freddy MacLennan not far behind, and the best centres have undoubtedly been Mike Gibson and Dick Milliken. I also have a high opinion of Michael Kiernan but I have always believed that Dick Milliken was good enough to have won fifty caps for Ireland if a serious leg injury had not ended his career at a young age. Gibson was the most complete player I ever came across. There was nothing that he could not do and he was, in short, a genius. He had a shrewd brain, a good defence, tremendous pace and level of fitness, a wicked dummy and side-step and he was a fabulous ball-player. He had the uncanny knack in any situation, no matter how tight or hopeless, of always doing the right thing. He had safe hands, kicked well with both feet and was always in the right place whether in support of an attack off the ball or cover tackling in the corner. He was unique and it was a richly rewarding experience to play with him on Lions tours and various select matches.

At full back I would put Hugo MacNeill just ahead of Tony Ensor, and add that as my first international against Tom Kiernan was his last for Ireland I did not consider him in making up this team. However, Kiernan was a highly successful coach of Ireland in 1982 and 1983 when he coached the backs with the redoubtable Syd Millar in charge of the forwards. I would make McBride captain, but apart from whipping up the pack beforehand his only other responsibility would be to toss up the coin prior to the match. On the field of play, Ollie Campbell and Mike Gibson would call all the shots, and Irish rugby could not be in safer hands. That would be a very strong Irish side, but the great thing about my friends across the sea is that, win or lose, the one thing that you could put your mortgage on is that we would have a night to remember afterwards, that is, if the next morning we could actually remember what had happened the night before. The Irish are always great crack and with the natural affinity between the Scots and the Irish we have shared a lot of fun together on various tours. The Scotland–Ireland matches may not always have been classics but they were keenly fought, packed full of raw commitment and good sportsmanship, and they were inevitably close and exciting. Whatever else, they led to some memorable evenings in Edinburgh and Dublin over the years.

6

The Free-Flowing French

My first game in the Five Nations Championship was against France in Paris in January 1973, and it happened to coincide with the first rugby international at the Parc des Princes stadium. Up to that time, the Paris matches had been played at Colombes but they were switched that season to the magnificent municipal ground at Parc des Princes which seats 50,000 supporters. The atmosphere is totally different there from any other ground in the world – a Dax band plays a musical accompaniment throughout the match, fire-crackers go off every minute, trumpets blare and the crowd becomes more and more vociferous and emotionally involved as the game progresses. The incredible noise gives the ear-drums an incessant battering, but I have never found it a hostile ground. Scotland have always enjoyed playing there and have been very popular visitors, although I have my suspicions that that might be tied up with the fact that in seven internationals in the new ground we have never won! It should be pointed out that the native attempt to unsettle the visiting team begins long before the fire-crackers, trumpets and the band sound off. The subtle brainwashing began on the Friday night when the team were taken to the Folies Bergères, and suitably placed in the best ringside seats to goggle at the performance. In the interval we were escorted backstage to be introduced to the gathering of stunningly beautiful, scantily clad dancers. As if that was not enough to divert our concentration from the might of the French forwards and the task in hand the next day, in the second half of the

87

show the girls invite a volunteer from the audience to join them on stage. With the Scottish team the guests of honour, as it were, and seated in pole position, it was inevitable that one of us would be the victim, if that is the right word in the rather special circumstances. I was the youngest member of the squad and before my feet touched the ground I was on centre stage, surrounded by 24 voluptuous, topless, dazzling females. I reckoned that thus far my first venture out of Scotland and into Europe was something of a success, and I was making a reasonable fist of displaying big match temperament in front of a large, cheering crowd. Surely the Parc des Princes would be a doddle after this. Glamorous girl after glamorous girl kissed me as I remained the focal point of attention while they danced round me, and I was having the time of my life. What I did not realize as I stood revelling in my little fantasy world was that the girls were made up with bright red lipstick which, after one kiss from each of them, left me grinning at the audience, festooned all over my face, neck and white shirt with 24 large, lip-shaped blobs of lipstick. The lads were jumping up and down in their seats, whistling and shouting as I posed on stage like the original Don Juan, and I assumed at the time that they were all consumed with jealousy at the young student hugging and kissing the most beautiful 24 girls in Paris. However, I realized later, of course, that they were beside themselves with laughter because the great Casanova from Goldenacre had ended up quite blissfully unaware that he looked a complete jerk, covered in lipstick.

Just in case that exotic experience was not sufficient to unnerve me and the rest of the team, the French swung into action with plan B after lunch the following day. The ride from our team hotel to the stadium is, as they say, something else. The cavalcade consists of our team bus, which I have a hunch is quite incidental to the whole exercise, and a dozen police cars and motor-cyclists. The scene looks as if it had been plucked straight from a Peter Sellers Pink Panther movie, with our bus hurtling through narrow Parisian side streets at about 60 miles per hour, closely pursuing the half a dozen police on motorbikes clearing the path. They seem to kick cars out of the way in the most aggressive and haphazard manner, and it is clearly a wonderful day's sport for them. I imagine there is no shortage of recruits when Inspector Clouseau asks for volunteers to help the Scotland team bus set a new world record time for crossing Paris in rush hour on the day of the international.

The stadium is usually a bright splash of colour, and contrary to popular opinion the supporters are knowledgeable and generous in their appreciation of rugby. If we opened out from our own goal-line as we did in 1973 and swept the length of the field, the French crowd would go wild with their hooters going full blast and the fire-crackers banging away twenty to the dozen. At the same time, they do not bend over backwards to see only the good in the French side through tricolour spectacles. France played pretty indifferent rugby in the opening 20 minutes that year, fumbling around in midfield in most uncharacteristic fashion. Then one of their centres was pole-axed in a tackle, I think it was Trillo, and the crowd as if one man began to chant 'Mazo, Mazo' for ages until the injured player recovered. Jo Mazo was the hero of the French public, with the suntanned good looks befitting a man who on more than one occasion appeared on the glossy covers of magazines such as *Paris Match*. He was also a fabulous player of the very highest quality who would rank in the top ten centres in world rugby in the past 20 years, and his omission from the team that year was most mysterious. Suspicions that he must have committed some cardinal sin off the pitch were confirmed by the fact that after 1973, though the best three-quarter in France, he never played in an international again.

The Parisian crowd was not interested in the political turmoil behind the scenes of the French federation; they simply wanted to see their idol brought on to the pitch to enliven a hitherto dull match. In fact, there were no more injuries, and the services of Mazo were not required as France, with Jean-Pierre Romeu kicking 12 points, squeezed home 16–13. Paris was littered later that night with several thousand kilted warriors who began the night upright and in agreement that France had just about deserved to win, but by the early hours of Sunday morning, having adopted a horizontal pose, felt that we had probably been robbed by the referee. Since the English referee, Ken Pattinson, injured a leg in the first quarter of an hour, and had to be replaced for the rest of the match by the French touch-judge, Francis Palmade, the fans might possibly have had something to moan about, but in fact any grievances had no foundation because Monsieur Palmade was admirably impartial and suitably strict. He did an excellent job, and became a top international referee from that moment right up to the present day.

Our hotel was in the centre of Paris, and both before and after the dinner we visited some of the nearby cafés to join in the festivities. It was great to find a batch of Scottish supporters wherever we went, thoroughly enjoying themselves, gargling with the local wine and bursting into song at any opportunity. I was boggle-eyed at the friendly atmosphere and genuine hospitality of the French. It is nice to report that the behaviour of the Scottish fans has always been good, though I have to admit that the odd person may have struggled to retain the considerable amount of wine consumed on the Saturday night. The dinner was held in the most magnificent dining hall of one of the plushest hotels in Paris, and the meal was a veritable banquet. Six superb courses were washed down with an unlimited quantity of top quality wine of every variety. I noted with approval that we each had six or seven glasses and, starting with an aperitif, we followed with white, rosé, and red wine, and rounded off the meal with port, brandy and liqueurs to ensure that every glass was gainfully employed. Unlike the domestic dinners after internationals, the

French soirée is mainly for the players. The French sing their favourite song and we reply with ours, and often they persuade one or two of their less introverted players to put on an impromptu cabaret. I can still see in my mind's eye Gérard Cholley and Robert Paparemborde, two large prop forwards specially dressed, or rather undressed, as Sumo wrestlers performing their own well-rehearsed but hilariously entertaining party piece. I enjoyed my five visits to France for internationals so much that it is the one away game that I will still attend every two years now that I have retired.

The only advantage of playing France at Murrayfield was the fact that we did manage the occasional isolated victory. In my time the first of these came in 1974, when we eventually ran out impressive winners, 19–6. Mind you, the French made a most auspicious start. The papers were full of chat beforehand about their new right wing three-quarter, Jean-François Gourdon. He was supposedly as fast as the speed of light. Our veteran campaigners assured the younger, more impressionable element that all the paper talk was exactly that – just paper talk. Greatly relieved that Gourdon, the blonde-haired Gallic god was merely mortal, we took the field. From the kick-off the ball was whipped along the visiting three-quarter line to their new wing. Gourdon accelerated round our left wing, Louis Dick, who was no slouch, as if he were a statue, and I suffered a similar indignity moments later. He flashed past the initial cover defence, and it was only when he cut back inside that he overreached his ambition and tripped over our covering forwards. He was, of course, to become an outstanding wing, but it was an early lesson for me of the strength and depth of French rugby, especially in their backs, which is unrivalled anywhere else. Their third, fourth or fifth best wing or full back would often be good enough to play for one of the home unions.

The French backs were usually a potent mixture of the unpredictable, the outrageous and the spectacular, but that day our pack overwhelmed them and we produced

91

all the clever running. It was a very satisfying day for me as I opened up twice from my own half to spark off tries which even the French would have been proud to have scored. The first contained a handling move which involved well over half our team interpassing before I was put through a gap to give the scoring pass to Alastair McHarg, skilfully positioned where a good wing three-quarter or an ambitious lock forward ought to have been. The second try began when I counter-attacked from my own half, and again most of the side handled before Louis Dick scored. I added two penalties and a conversion and played with the sort of confidence which only comes with the knowledge that I was now established in the Scotland side.

The next five years belonged to France as they recorded wins of differing margins. Only in 1975 might we have won. That was the closest we have ever come to beating France at Parc des Princes. We lost 10–9 but I narrowly missed with a drop at goal and six penalty kicks out of nine. The last, in the final five minutes, was the simplest of all, but I hooked it from 30 yards just wide of the upright. It was the sort of kick I would expect to slot nine times out of ten, and it was a depressing end to a depressing match which featured far too many outbursts of fighting among the forwards and too little rugby of any quality. Had any one of my missed penalties been successful we would have shared the Championship that season with Wales, but even worse was to follow in 1976.

We lost to France at Murrayfield and that was the first home defeat I had suffered in a Scottish jersey since my first cap four years earlier. This was the season that saw the emergence of the formidable French side which, along with Wales, was to dominate five of the next six seasons. The front row of Cholley, Paco and Paparemborde was like a mobile brick wall, and they mopped up the loose ball with three players who were fabulous both individually and as a back-row unit – Rives, Bastiat and Skrela. With Bertranne, Sangali and Gourdon in the three-quarter line they were well on their way to

Removing the straw at Murrayfield for yet another squad session

Playing for the French Barbarians in Biarritz against the All Blacks

Sir Geoffrey Howe gave away very little as Chancellor but the Quins Sevens Trophy belonged to Heriot's in 1979

Bang goes another for Heriot's at Goldenacre

One of my proudest moments – holding the Schweppes Trophy when Heriot's won the League title in 1979

Counter-attacking at Murrayfield from near the Scottish line

Tony Neary should have won more England caps and played in more Lions Tests

Fair odds – one Scot, Renwick, against two Englishmen, Beaumont and Uttley

Sid Going – New Zealand's answer to Gareth Edwards

New Zealand's Bruce Robertson, supported by Bill Osborne, a dynamic
pairing

Fergus Slattery, a brilliant success with the Lions in 1974, sorely missed in 1977 and 1980

Bill Beaumont and myself at Easter Road, the Hibs football ground, prior to a Calcutta Cup match

My first try for Scotland in 1974 against the Auld Enemy

On stage at the Folies Bergères on my first trip to Paris in 1973

A friendly Maori welcome to New Zealand in 1977. The All Blacks were less friendly

Spot the tourists in New Zealand in 1981. Jim Telfer's training sessions were not quite such a laugh

On top of Table Mountain in Cape Town, J.P.R., J.J. Williams and myself check to see Phil Bennett has no grey hairs

Touring is not all hard work as John Beattie and I discovered on the beach in Durban

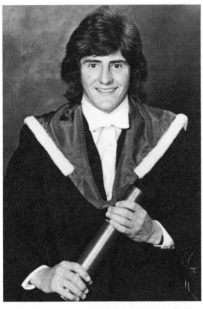

Graduation from Edinburgh University in 1973, proving that long-haired students could read and write

Outside Buckingham Palace with my M B E in 1979

Meeting the Queen before the Calcutta Cup match at Murrayfield in 1976

Audrey, Sara and Jennie welcome me
back from Australia

Audrey with our first daughter aged one
day – this photo was wired to me in
Hamilton, New Zealand, in 1977

Mark Loane, a world-class number 8, under pressure from Milne, Leslie, Aitken and Laidlaw

Phil Bennett shows his wizadry en route to scoring his spectacular try in 1977

A great player and a great friend –
Jim Renwick

Rives not exactly feeling sorry for
Scotland after scoring against us
in 1982

My last Five Nations match for Scotland when we beat Wales 34-18 in 1982

John Rutherford beats Peter Winterbottom on a typical break

Will four Frenchmen be enough to stop David Leslie?

A farewell reception at Edinburgh airport before leaving for Australia in 1982

The eight Heriot's full backs who played for Scotland: Ian Thomson, Colin Blaikie, Jimmy Kerr, Jimmy Gray, Ken Scotland, Ian Smith, myself and Dan Drysdale

Hard luck, Jack – keep practising

Who says this wee man is not strong. The lads failed to emulate Gary Player's feat

becoming unstoppable. None the less we missed eight kicks at goal in the first half with a strong wind behind us and another one in the second half which meant we squandered 27 possible points. Dougie Morgan failed with four and I missed five, although I should point out that the referee made a horrendous blunder to deprive us of three points when we were already 3–0 in the lead.

In the gusting, swirling wind, our captain Ian McLauchlan held the ball steady for me for a long-range penalty from about the French ten-yard line. He was positioned slightly in front of the ball which is, according to law 27 (d), perfectly permissible. I knew full well that the person holding the ball was allowed to be exactly where McLauchlan was, and I was astounded after I struck the ball a mighty thump, and saw the two touch-judges raise their flags in the air to signify the goal had been kicked, that the referee, Ken Pattinson, disallowed the three points because he claimed McLauchlan was technically offside. He gave a scrum to France much to our surprise, displeasure and disappointment. There is no telling if our run of ten consecutive home wins would have been extended if that penalty had been allowed as it should have been. What I do know is that the majority of top referees, if they had thought McLauchlan really was technically offside, would have probably felt it was within the spirit of the game to quietly mention it. It was, as Pattinson humbly admitted afterwards, a bad decision by any standards.

Funnily enough, our referee the following year in Paris was also in charge of his last international, but I would hasten to add that in my opinion Meirion Joseph was vastly superior to Pattinson. The problem that day was that an extremely talented French team resorted to an unwarranted, physical brutality that ruined the spectacle and soured a victory which happened to be their biggest ever against Scotland. Gérard Cholley began the match by punching Donald MacDonald flush on the jaw and laying him out. He should have been sent off there and then. Amazingly he survived that incident and two more when he meted out similar rough, totally unprovoked and unnecessary treatment on Jim Renwick and Ron Wilson. Mr Joseph warned Cholley and penalized him but disregarding the good of the game and the image of rugby, he neglected to send Cholley off. In fairness, even with fourteen men, France would probably have won because not only were they in the ascendency, but our venerable pack of the mid-seventies was beginning to decline. 1977 was the turning point, and we were in for four lean years during which time we finished bottom of the Championship table three times and second bottom once. Sandy Carmichael was coming to the end of his career, Gordon Brown was banned by the Scottish Rugby Union for three months at Christmas and never played for Scotland again, David Leslie was injured and out for two seasons, and with McHarg reverting from No. 8 to lock to replace Brown, our back row was vulnerable.

Our pack was comprehensively outplayed and yet, in these adverse circumstances, I reckoned I played just about my best match for Scotland. I spent most of the 80 minutes tackling but still managed to launch a handful of attacks as well, and considering how we were hopelessly outdone by the French, I think we emerged with some credit. That was the third leg of the French Grand Slam that season, but instead of jubilant celebrations at the dinner, their President, Albert Ferrasse, severely reprimanded Cholley and warned him that a recurrence of his over-aggressive play would mean that he would never again represent France. Such a speech reflected little credit on Meirion Joseph, but the truth is that if Gordon Brown or my mum had been in charge we would still have lost, so much stronger and better were the French. I always had the highest regard for Meirion both as a referee and as a person, and after such a distinguished career I felt genuinely sorry it had to end in a controversial manner. For all the wonderful quality of the best French teams in recent years, I think it is worth pointing out that they have also been guilty of dirty play on far too many occasions, and this has greatly detracted from their overall impressive record. Not only the Scottish forwards, but most international players with whom I have mixed in the home unions have regularly felt that the French were the dirtiest team they ever played against – and that includes teams from the southern hemisphere.

I would hate to put the *entente cordiale* in danger and it would be churlish to keep making excuses for our defeats by France, but in 1978 we were once again the victims of wretched luck. In bucketing rain, the French found the alien conditions far from their liking and they were in disarray and showing a singular lack of commitment as we raced to a lead of 13 points. However, in chasing the ball from my own 25 to the French goal-line, despite blatant obstruction and jersey-pulling by Gourdon, and winning the race for the touch-down to score our second try of the game, I damaged my acromio-clavicular joint. I played only a further two minutes of the match, being replaced by a centre three-quarter, Alastair Cranston. From 13–0 up, we lost 19–16.

The match in 1979 was one of the best games of the decade. Each side scored three smashing tries in a thrilling display of running rugby. Both sides adopted a bold, almost foolhardy, attacking policy and, as if it were an infectious disease, everyone threw the ball around in the most exciting manner. This was John Rutherford's first season for Scotland and he made a huge difference to our range of attacking options. It was disappointing to lose such a fabulous game but it was still an immensely enjoyable, incredibly open exhibition of everything that is good in rugby. I had managed to score one try that year in Paris, and in 1980 at Murrayfield in an equally marvellous match which produced another two tries, I scored two in an international for the first and only time in my career. The Scottish victory that afternoon ended a disastrous run of 13 games without a win, and the manner of our triumph was quite remarkable. All's well that ends well, but I must confess that I had a Jekyll and Hyde match with the first hour resembling an unbelievable nightmare. I missed my simplest penalty kick in a Scottish jersey from 15 yards out almost in front of the posts, but ended up scoring 16 points altogether which was a new individual Scottish record in a full inter-national. I missed several kicks at goal in the first half which led to large sections of the crowd barracking me and demanding a change of kicker. That was all very disturbing, and matters became even more serious early in the second half when France opened up a lead of 14–4.

We trailed by ten points right up to the final twelve minutes of the game, and then, suddenly, dramatically, we exploded into action, throwing caution to the winds, running everything, attacking non-stop and launching the most sensational recovery in the Five Nations Championship in my time. We rattled up 18 points without reply to turn a 14–4 deficit into a sensational 22–14 success. We created two of the very best tries scored at Murrayfield which even the French would have been thrilled to emulate. I opened up from my own half and the majority of our side handled and supported the ball as we switched from defence to attack, catching the opposition a little flat-footed. I was up in the line again to round off the move with a try in the corner, and I inflicted another shock on the French supporters, who had earlier written me off as a liability to Scotland, when I added the conversion from the touch-line. Six minutes later, another inspirational bout of interpassing between the backs and the forwards engineered an overlap in which John Rutherford, David Johnston and Jim Ren-wick cut out most of the running. For the second time in six minutes we had run France ragged, and I was the lucky man, having sprinted up from the back to join the movement, who happened to be in the right place at the right time to gratefully accept the scoring pass and touch down near the posts. Jim Renwick added the conversion while I got my breath back (16–14) and in the dying minutes I kicked two penalties to leave the French feeling like beached whales, trying to get their breath back and work out what had gone so horribly wrong for

them. 22–14. It was an extraordinary reversal of fortunes.

I cannot remember so many points being scored in an
international in such a short space of time to turn certain
defeat into glorious victory. The two happiest players
afterwards were Colin Deans and myself. Colin was
winning his eleventh cap after three years in the Scottish
team and yet this was his first time in a winning side. As
for me, my only wish at half-time was to sneak off home
in the hope that no one would notice. By the middle of
the second half, after further disasters had befallen me, I
thought I was probably playing my last game for
Scotland. I reckoned I would be replaced at full back by
Bruce Hay for the next match or Ron Wilson or Ken
Scotland or even, if a hundred others fell by the wayside,
by Dan Drysdale, who was amazingly sprightly for a
septuagenarian and had collected his last cap as recently
as 1929. Happily the last 20 minutes were ample
compensation for the earlier torment and agony, and in
the final analysis it was a fairy-tale ending. That French
match in 1980 was certainly not my favourite game but
the final 12 minutes would count as my favourite 12
consecutive minutes of rugby ever.

My last two appearances against France reverted to
normal and were most notable for my improved good
fortune as a goal kicker. In our defeat in 1981 the solitary
penalty goal I landed that day meant that I had set a
new world record for 213 points in international rugby
which beat Phil Bennett's previous record of 210 points,
but a win over France that afternoon would have meant
far more to me. In 1982, I had the satisfaction of landing
three more penalties and of captaining Scotland to a
victory over France for only the third such win in ten
matches. For the next triumph, in 1984, I was sitting in
my tracksuit in the old stand acting as a replacement
while Scotland completed the Grand Slam for only the
second time this century. It was a magnificent, Scottish
rearguard performance, but certainly not a day the
French will recall with any affection. They were undisci-

plined beyond reason and channelled more energy into arguing with the referee and disputing his decisions than they did into attempting to overcome Scotland. They did not do themselves justice that day and they paid the penalty, literally and metaphorically.

Unfortunately that particular occasion was not an isolated example of the temperamental fragility of the French team when they were rattled and under pressure playing away from Paris. However, there was a period under the captaincy of Jacques Fouroux when they seemed to instil in their attitude a new discipline and organization which, allied to their natural skill and flamboyance, helped them to win the Championship in 1977 and challenge hard as the runners-up in 1976, 1978 and 1979. Of all the sides in the Championship, indeed of all the international board countries, I preferred to play against France more than any other because they play the best and most attractive rugby and always try not just to win but to win in style. There is little or none of the relentless, grinding forward play so typical of New Zealand and South Africa, or even England and Wales, and they scarcely ever resort to the kick-and-chase tactics – or really lack of tactics – which so many countries pursue in the northern hemisphere and which makes a Five Nations match or an international against Romania look like a play-off in the European Up-and-Under Championship. The French are the most delightfully creative and artistic of sides, packed full of gifted footballers not only in the backs but also in the pack. They can all run and pass and react quickly to any situation, and their instinctive willingness to play open rugby makes them excellent supporters of the man with the ball and extremely dangerous opponents.

One great advantage they enjoy over British players is the weather. The playing conditions in the South of France are invariably vastly preferable to the mud, wind, rain, snow and frost of Scotland from November through to February. Such conditions invite good rugby and it is impossible to emphasize too strongly the huge difference which the weather makes. Over and over again, critics complain about the standard of matches taking place on appalling days without fully appreciating that it is virtually impossible to produce a decent game in such adverse circumstances. The worse the weather, the easier it is for the poorer side to succeed with purely destructive and negative tactics and, of course, the corollary is also true. I would have loved my rugby even more if Goldenacre could have been whisked away on a magic carpet to the South of France every Saturday during my career. Good playing conditions automatically raise the standard, and pundits should never forget or ignore this fact.

It is also worth pointing out that the *laissez-faire* attitude of French referees also helps promote entertaining rugby. I loved playing under the likes of Georges Domercq or Jean-Pierre Bonnet or Francis Palmade. The liberally minded referees of France seem to share a splendid sense of discretion which punishes the major infringements, especially in the fiercely competitive club championship matches, which ensures a tight control of potentially explosive confrontations, and yet encourages an open brand of play by excellent use of the advantage law and the more questionable Lord Nelson approach to the fractional forward pass or marginal knock-on. Research shows that a large number of the most exciting, free-flowing major matches have been handled by French referees.

This background of good weather, good coaching, naturally skilful and dedicated footballers, a first-class club structure and benevolent referees has been responsible for the improvement of French rugby in the 1970s and the 1980s. The French have also realized the importance of sound tackling and good defensive play, which was often conspicuously absent in the not-so-good old days. As a result they could muster a tremendous composite team from the past twelve years with only one position showing a noticeable lack of strength. They have never had a brilliant fly half and more often than not have selected some very average performers in this crucial position. With so many talented three-quarters the mind boggles at the mouth-watering prospect of a three-quarter line of, say, Jean-François Gourdon, Roland Bertranne, Didier Codorniou and Serge Blanco or Jean-Luc Averous being sparked off by a fly half like Barry John, Phil Bennett, John Rutherford, Ollie Campbell or Mark Ella. The best they have had recently has been Jean-Pierre Romeu, but he was really no more than an adequate journeyman, and they have had some very indifferent operators indeed like Paries, Vives, Aguerre, Caussade, Laporte, Pedeutour, Didier Camberabero and Lescarboura. It has been a glaring deficiency which is all the more surprising when you consider the strength in depth of the rest of the French team.

In my view, Jean-Michel Aguirre has been the best full back, a player able to adapt to any game plan and adopt any given role, and Jérôme Gallion is an excellent scrum half with a wide-ranging repertoire. Not many front rows would get the better of Gérard Cholley, Phillipe Dintrans and Robert Paparemborde. With not many outstanding line-out jumpers, there is a strong argument for picking two players who were outstanding scrummagers, ruckers and maulers who were mobile in the loose and could run and handle too – Michel Palmie and Alain Esteve fit the bill. From a dozen top-class back-row forwards I would choose Jean-Pierre Rives, Jean-Pierre Bastiat and Jean-Claude Skrela, with Jean-Luc Joinel on the bench, desperately unlucky to be left out.

Rives would be captain of this team which is of the highest class and would be ideally suited to maintaining their tradition of playing their own very special brand of fluent rugby. Such a XV would be almost unbeatable if they could maintain self-discipline and eliminate temperamental outbursts. Those moments of hot-headedness not only give away penalties but have the more far-reaching effect of unsettling the whole rhythm of the side. Without any doubt, it cost France two of their three defeats by Scotland in my memory – 1982 and 1984 they were the better side, but lost. I have no sympathy for them. With the two unbeaten sides in the Championship clashing in the final match of the season in 1984, and with the Grand Slam automatically on a plate for the victors, they knew what was at stake. I have to be honest and say that France were the superior side that day but by their perpetual petulance and indiscipline they came off second best against the tenacity and single-minded determination and dedication of the Scots. The big difference between the Grand Slam sides of France in 1977, Wales in 1978 and England in 1980, the Irish Triple Crown side of 1982 and the Scottish Grand Slam side of 1984 is that if the Championship in each of these five seasons had been replayed ten times then France, Wales and England would have still been top of the tree at least nine, if not ten times out of ten. On the other hand, Ireland and Scotland might only have repeated their particular triumphs three or four times out of the ten. The fact is that France at the present time are carrying the flag for European rugby most regularly and most consistently in the eighties, and because of their natural, inherent strengths compared to the general weakness which has afflicted the four home unions after the heady days of the early and mid-seventies, there is every reason to suspect that France will be at, or near, the head of affairs in the northern hemisphere in the immediate future.

7

The Extraordinary All Blacks

My first match against New Zealand was a very special game for me because it was my first cap for Scotland. Similarly, my first tour to New Zealand in 1975 was equally special because I met my eldest brother, Bill, for the first time and was reunited with my other brother, Jim, for the first time since the early sixties. Bill had left home to join the Merchant Navy at the age of 17 at around the time I was born. Jim, who is just one year younger than Bill, left Edinburgh to work in London in the mid-fifties when I was only five, and in 1963 he also emigrated to New Zealand. If I have one major regret in my rugby career it is that my immediate family saw only five of my 51 internationals between them. Tragically, my father, who worked most of his life as an engineer in Africa and who would have loved to see me playing rugby, was killed in a car accident in Nigeria in 1967. Although he was primarily a soccer supporter, he had followed my early career at Heriot's school, and had seen me playing occasionally when he had been home on leave, but sadly he was never to see me play for Scotland.

The first time my two brothers were to see me in an international was in June 1975 in Auckland, and it was the double prospect of meeting my brothers and meeting the All Blacks again which made the trip to New Zealand so important and significant to me. We flew to New Zealand via Hong Kong and Sydney, and when the plane touched down at Auckland airport, Bill, his wife and five children were there to greet me. It was a strange sensation trying to come to terms with the fact that I was actually an uncle to their two boys and three girls, and to realize that my brother, sister-in-law and nieces and nephews all had strong New Zealand accents. We exchanged gossip briefly before heading off for the venue of our opening match at Nelson where Jim and his wife were waiting for us. We spent happy hours during the next three days trying the best we could to fill in the countless gaps in the previous 20-odd years, and we met up again in the latter part of that short tour when Scotland returned to the north part of North Island for the final two matches in Rotorua and Auckland. Happily I was to meet up from time to time with Bill, Jim and their families again during the Lions tour to New Zealand in 1977.

Unfortunately, the international against New Zealand in 1975 was not the ideal match for my brothers to watch me for the first time. The conditions were, without a shadow of a doubt, the worst I have ever played in, and had it been a match in the Five Nations Championship it would have certainly been postponed. That weekend Auckland was subjected to one of the most continuous torrential downpours in its history. Heavy rain began to fall on Friday around lunchtime, and it continued unabated all afternoon, all evening, all night and all Saturday morning with over four inches falling in those few hours. By kick-off there were several large lakes on the pitch with four or five inches of water lying on top of the ground which meant it was positively dangerous to play rugby. Anybody trapped face down in a pool of water at the bottom of a ruck would be in danger of drowning, but it was decided to play in the knowledge that the referee might have to blow up rucks and mauls early if a player was submerged at any time and unable to move.

It rained right through the match, and as if that was not bad enough there was a strong wind blowing almost straight behind New Zealand in the first half. At the interval they led only 6–0 with a try by Hamish Macdonald which was converted by Joe Karam, and at

103

that point with the advantage of the considerable elements to follow, everything pointed to a first ever Scottish win over the All Blacks. Incredibly, those hopes were rapidly dashed. Having played into the teeth of the gale and been lashed by the icy rain for 40 minutes, while we stood sucking our oranges at half-time the wind veered right round and we had the remarkable misfortune to play into the wind and the driving rain again in the second half. Bryan Williams scored two tries, and Duncan Robertson one and, showing rare skill in the appalling conditions, Joe Karam converted all three to give the All Blacks their biggest win over Scotland up to that point, 24–0.

My next two matches against the All Blacks for Scotland were in 1978 and 1979 on their superb Grand Slam tour and the short tour of Scotland and England the following year. Graham Mourie's Grand Slam side were a magnificent all-round team without a single weakness and tremendous strength in depth. They had a few players who could not make their Test side but who would have been welcomed with open arms by the home unions at the time. They had an outstanding coach in the late Jack Gleeson, and they played good rugby whatever the conditions. We did our best to make them feel at home at Murrayfield, coming fairly close to the water polo at Auckland in 1975 except that there was no water actually lying on the pitch. It rained persistently during the game, and towards the end it became very dark. Although New Zealand were the better side and seemingly well in control, they only led 12–9 as the game moved into injury time, and we were on the attack in their 25 when the ball came to Ian McGeechan. Three months of hard work was on the verge of coming to nothing – the victories over Ireland (10–6), Wales (13–12) and England (16–6) were about to be rendered merely individual achievements rather than being three-quarters of a first ever Grand Slam in Britain and Ireland as McGeechan lined up a drop at goal to level the scores. In desperation Doug Bruce, the All Blacks fly half, darted forward and charged down the kick. I was up in the Scottish line expecting a handling movement and hoping to create the extra man for the winning try which meant all the Scottish backs were moving forward as the ball cannoned off Bruce back over the New Zealand 25. Bill Osborne, their centre, swooped onto it to hack it up to the half-way line and then, in the gathering gloom, the lights went out for Scotland as Bruce Robertson proceeded to kick and chase to our goal-line where he touched down for the try that clinched the match and gave Mourie's All Blacks a well-deserved place in history.

The following year with nine different players in their side they ran out comfortable winners by 20–6, scoring four tries to none. Two of the tries were scored by new young players who were to be crucial to the continued run of success which New Zealand sustained during the next six seasons – scrum half Dave Loveridge and No. 8 Murray Mexted.

My final two matches against New Zealand were in 1981 when I captained Scotland on an eight-match tour there. In the first Test at Dunedin we created enough chances to win with John Rutherford at fly half making several tremendous breaks late in the second half to stretch the All Blacks cover to the limit. The crucial moment, however, came when Loveridge scored an infuriatingly simple try when we heeled the ball at a scrum on our own line, and the New Zealand scrum half dived in amongst all the Scottish feet to touch down, quite legally, for the try. It was the sort of quick-thinking opportunism and instinctive reflex action which has helped to make Loveridge one of the best scrum halves in the last decade. With renewed confidence from the cushion of seven points – Hewson had kicked a first-half penalty – New Zealand quickly launched another, more ambitious attack and Stu Wilson scored a try. In the last quarter of an hour we hit back dramatically with non-stop running and handling which really rocked the All Blacks back on their heels. Our only try was scored by

Colin Deans but Jim Renwick, John Rutherford and Steve Munro came perilously close to scoring three more, and at the end the home players admitted they were very relieved to hear the final whistle.

We felt that we finished that match right on top, and there was more optimism before the second Test in Auckland than I could ever recall when playing against New Zealand. Indeed there was one moment mid-way through the second half when we had a chance to take control, and New Zealand were definitely flustered. It was a magnificent game of running rugby with a great deal of exceptionally skilful play and a whole series of breathtaking moves. At half-time the All Blacks led 10–6 and early in the second half they increased that margin to 22–6. Our recovery was immediate, inspirational and so very nearly overwhelming. Bruce Hay scored a try which I converted, and I also kicked a penalty to make it 22–15. At that point we twice in the space of four minutes seemed certain to score tries by the posts which would have given us a five-point lead with 20 minutes left. I have always argued that almost every international has a turning point no matter what the final score is, that the outcome depends on one or perhaps two incidents. This match, despite the final large margin of New Zealand's victory, was no exception. Trailing 22–15, Steve Munro was put completely clear but after spending the previous 48 hours in bed with flu, our flying wing was caught from behind by Bernie Fraser who made up the best part of ten yards to prevent Munro touching down. Shortly after this, we won three rucks in succession and Jim Calder touched down for what seemed to be a perfectly good try. Of the 44,000 people watching, the referee, Mr Collett from Australia, was the only person to detect a forward pass. This decision baffled and demoralized us.

We sustained our offensive for another ten minutes without reward, and then the All Blacks scored three tries at the end from Allan Hewson, Stu Wilson and Bruce Robertson which were all converted by Hewson to wrap up the game. The final score of 40–15 sounds like a massacre, but I honestly believe that if Munro and Calder had scored their tries we might have sprung a surprise. That may sound like outrageous optimism and in the final analysis there is no denying that New Zealand were worthy winners of a wonderful match, but the losing margin of 25 points did scant justice to Scotland's performance.

That was my tenth and last game against New Zealand at international level, and I was left with just one win in ten years, and that was the Lions victory in the Second Test at Christchurch in 1977. There are many reasons why a country with a population of just three million consistently produces the best rugby team in the world. First of all, rugby is far and away the major sport in New Zealand. Every male who has any sporting ability at all plays rugby. If that happened in Britain we would produce very much better international sides, but our resources are spread much more thinly, for rugby competes with a whole range of other sports. In New Zealand virtually every school in the country specializes in rugby, and the standard of coaching and the emphasis on the basic skills is without parallel anywhere in the world. They start at the age of five, and within two or three years all the boys can do all the simple things well. The youngsters are lucky that they do not have too many counter-attractions to distract them. New Zealand television is, as yet, scarcely a worthy opponent to a rugby ball on a sunny afternoon, and I was interested to learn from all the schools I visited in my various stints in New Zealand that between the end of school each day and suppertime, the vast majority prefer playing with a rugby ball to watching television or doing anything else. The combination of keen schoolmasters, excellent coaching and competitive leagues from an early age helps to develop the best in the boys to prepare them for the challenges ahead. They are technically well equipped, and it is the dream of almost every self-respecting New Zealander to play one day for the All Blacks. There is nothing quite comparable in sport in Britain.

An All Black rugby player is afforded almost film-star status, and the papers, radio and television all give rugby top priority. With this very privileged position in society, it is not surprising that the New Zealand rugby player is a very dedicated, determined individual. With such extensive competition to reach the top, those who succeed are extremely tough, big, strong, ruthless guys who have to beat off the challenges of players whom the home unions would be thrilled to have at their disposal. It is the survival of the fittest, the strongest, the best and the most determined. The average New Zealander reaches a far greater degree of fitness than we do, and he invariably takes his rugby far more seriously. They virtually never have a bad player in an All Blacks jersey in an international. Compare that to the home championship in 1985 when nearly half of every side was made up of very average players who would not sniff a game for New Zealand in a lifetime. It is an indictment on the current parlous state of British rugby that in the final match of a desperately moderate Championship, I doubt if more than half a dozen of the 30 players representing Wales and England at Cardiff would get even close to the current New Zealand squad. That leaves, by New Zealand's high standards, 24 sub-par players.

I admire immensely their phenomenal devotion to rugby, and they richly deserve their long-standing success. It was best summed up for me by Ken Stewart, the flanker on the tour over here in 1979, who explained how he monitored his weight and level of fitness every day during the tour and often put in extra training at 9 or 10 o'clock in the evening to make sure he would withstand the challenge from the other wing forwards on the trip.

It is interesting too to note how their tight forwards are more athletic and better footballers generally than the front five forwards at home. We may have outscrummaged them in 1977 and on other occasions, but a fat lot of good it did us in the long run. They are not just technically superior but they are far more committed because winning at rugby means more to them than it does to us. They produce backs built like tanks who are fleet-footed and brilliant footballers as well, like Bryan Williams, Bruce Robertson, Bill Osborne, Bernie Fraser and Stu Wilson. If everything else has let them down at any time, they can always rely on their pride to pull them through. They say in New Zealand that it is the ambition of every young boy to play for the All Blacks, and it is the ambition of every young girl to marry an All Black. When New Zealand play an international against Scotland at Murrayfield in the afternoon, it is 3 o'clock in the morning back in New Zealand. Yet it is estimated that two million out of the three million population get up in the middle of the night to listen to live commentary on the radio. That further demonstrates the amazing intensity of feeling which All Black rugby inspires. They were the top rugby-playing country in the world when I played my first match in 1972, and they were still at the top in 1984 when I retired, and, all things considered, I'm not the slightest bit surprised. From so many great players, I suggest this team would be good enough to win a World Cup over the past dozen years. Full back, Bevan Wilson; the wings, Stu Wilson and Bryan Williams; centres, Bruce Robertson and Bill Osborne; half-backs, Duncan Robertson and Sid Going; front row, Brad Johnstone, Andy Dalton, Gary Knight; locks, Andy Haden and Frank Oliver; back row, Graham Mourie, Murray Mexted and Ian Kirkpatrick. The daunting fact is that they could pick a second, third, fourth and possibly fifth XV which would be not that far behind the side named above.

8

The Wallabies

Although I only managed one victory in ten games against New Zealand, I was on the winning side in four of the five matches I played for Scotland against Australia, and I feel that sums up the difference between these two fiercely competitive countries. Their rivalry goes back to the turn of the century, but despite Australia's recent highly successful tour to Britain, the facts speak for themselves, and in 78 internationals against New Zealand, Australia have only won 19 times up to 1985.

The problem in Australia is very similar to that in Britain. Rugby Union is not the number one national sport, and the Wallabies have to go out into the market-place to compete for players. There is no doubt in my mind that if everyone in Australia who played rugby league, Aussie rules, Australian football and the various other winter team games switched to rugby union they would be the best country in the world nine years out of ten. They have certain natural advantages like the weather which is conducive to good rugby and encourages the handling, running game at which they excel. As a race the Australians are tough, physical, aggressive, sports-loving people, and rugby union is the perfect game for them. But because the rich, natural playing resources of the country are divided amongst several conflicting winter sports, rugby union probably attracts less than a quarter of the potentially outstanding rugby union players to the game.

The main problem up until the tour of Andy Slack's

side over here in 1984 has been their inability to produce really good, rugged front five forwards with a reasonably sound set-piece technique. They have produced a never-ending list of great backs but their tight forwards have consistently let them down. I also believe that though they thoroughly deserved their success in sweeping through Britain and Ireland in 1984 to complete their first ever Grand Slam over here, and though they played some magical rugby *en route*, the success of their pack is only relative to the sharp decline in standards over here. Admittedly, the Australians were more solid than hitherto, and had a few really tall locks to guarantee line-out ball, but the domination achieved by the Australians in the four internationals has to be measured against the poor sides they beat. They still lost in the summer of 1984 to an under-strength New Zealand side in a series in Sydney and Brisbane, and they are still some way short of outplaying the All Blacks up front even if they can boast a more exciting, more talented back division at the moment.

In 1975, the first time I played Australia, they arrived at Murrayfield having lost only two of their first 11 matches on that tour, but their pack were well beaten by Scotland that day, and it was only their resolute defence which kept the winning margin down to 10–3. Their front five forwards were inadequate in the tight, and lost three of the four internationals on that tour, their sole success coming against Ireland.

Things had not changed all that much the next time I played against them on their next British tour in 1981. As in 1975, they beat Ireland, but lost to Wales, Scotland and England, although the Scottish result caused a great deal of heated argument. We won by 24 points to 15, which may look convincing enough but the Wallabies scored three tries to our one and felt they were very unlucky to lose in such circumstances. I landed five penalties that afternoon, and converted our only try by Jim Renwick, but I was still upset after the game at our performance. I have long felt that the side scoring the most tries should win, but when I analysed that particular match I felt the Australians could, in so many ways, only blame themselves.

I learned that evening that my 17 points was a new Scottish record by an individual in an international but it meant very little to me, and I would have willingly swapped all those penalties for a couple of extra tries by any of our backs. However, I must point out that in all probability we would have scored at least three more tries if the Australians had not given away so many penalties for offside at rucks and killing the ball in the loose when we were on the attack, driving forward, setting up good second-phase possession and on one occasion third-phase ball, with double overlaps screaming to score when the Wallabies transgressed the laws. I would argue vociferously that if they had not infringed the laws and the spirit of the game in those instances we would have won loose possession with extra men in the line, and I would state, as certain as one can be in such a situation, that we would very probably have scored at least two and probably three tries. The fact that I kicked five penalties and they scored more tries does not automatically mean that they were robbed. They gave away penalties rather than tries, and paid the consequence for such indiscretions. At the final reckoning they must shoulder much of the blame themselves for gross indiscipline.

Having said that, they did create two splendid tries. The first of these came after I had foolishly tried to open up from my own 25, and a long pass from me which was intended for Roger Baird went astray. He retreated rapidly, fell on the ball near our line and after half of the Australian team descended on him and he was engulfed in gold jerseys, the final insult came when he was penalized for not releasing the ball. However, instead of kicking the goal, Paul McLean floated a long diagonal punt 40 yards across the face of our goal wide to the left wing where Brendan Moon soared above Keith Robertson's outstretched hands to catch the ball and fall over the line for an amazing try. It was the sort of ambitious, ingenious split-second thinking and skilful reaction which deserves to win a game, and the try by Andy Slack soon after was of the same quality. It was a delightfully creative try involving some slick interpassing between Mark Ella, Moon and Slack, and was the best movement of the match. On the other hand, our try was largely a scrambled, untidy affair when Roger Gould misjudged a high kick, and Jim Renwick hit the jackpot with a lucky bounce to score. There is no denying the quality of their tries and I must confess it was very hard not to feel sympathy for them in defeat, but the fact remains that in their overenthusiastic defence of their goal-line they were far too quick to give away penalties rather than allow tries, and one or two of their leading players acknowledged this in private afterwards. They defended their line at any cost and that cost was pretty high. In the four internationals they gave away 45 points through kicks. I landed five penalties, Tony Ward managed four for Ireland, Gwyn Evans three for Wales and Marcus Rose three for England. They outscored England by two tries to one, Wales by two tries to one and Scotland by three tries to one but lost all three matches through penalty goals.

My last two games against Australia were, as it turned out, my last two internationals. We won the first in Brisbane in July 1982 by 12 points to 7 which had some added significance because I was winning my 50th cap to equal the Scottish record set by Sandy Carmichael. Much more importantly, I was captaining Scotland to a first success in a full international in the southern hemisphere. It was a particularly satisfying win after our heavy defeats two weeks earlier by both Queensland and Sydney. The coach, Jim Telfer, John Rutherford and myself spent an evening analysing what went wrong in those games and realized that with their slick passing and use of a running full back and blind-side wing in attack we were too often outnumbered. For the Test we brought our flanker, Jim Calder, out to fly half in

113

defensive situations on their ball, and moved all the backs out one which worked a treat in stifling their running rugby. Our pack was good enough to hold them with seven forwards, and they failed to create the sort of overlaps which had beaten us previously on the tour. A try by Keith Robertson, a drop goal by John Rutherford and a penalty and a conversion by me was just enough to help us make history, but I would be the first to say that Australia were the more attractive side that day. If the spectacle had been marked à la Torville and Dean, for artistic merit, then we would have been soundly beaten, but we tackled and covered superbly and took our chances well. We had been real underdogs but we rose to the occasion and it was an immensely satisfying result. That match, incidentally, was the first international to be played by Scotland on a Sunday, but the following Saturday Australia picked a stronger team and played top quality, open rugby. They hammered us by 33 points to 9. Their pack did much better in the second Test, and their backs tore us apart. It was a performance of outstanding merit and a foretaste of what they were going to achieve in Britain two years later. Their backs run straight and hard, unlike so many British sides who drift aimlessly across the field, and the Australian passing is quicksilver and deadly. They run off the ball and support each other so well that when things are going their way they are a joy to watch. Other teams throughout the world can only learn from them.

It was obviously disappointing to lose my last game for Scotland, but at least I went out to a team playing exactly the style and brand of rugby that I loved to play myself throughout my career, and I'm delighted that they have enjoyed so much success since that game. They have had problems up front but they have had plenty of world class backs since I played against them in 1975. My best Australian selection since then would comprise an excellent back division and an adequate pack. It would be: full back, Roger Gould; wings, Paddy Batch and Brendan Moon; centres, Michael Hawker and

Michael O'Connor; half-backs, Paul McLean and John Hipwell; front row, John Meadows, Peter Horton and Tony D'Arcy; locks, Garrick Fay and Steve Williams; back row, Tony Shaw, Mark Loane and Simon Poidevin.

If they could develop a pack to match the ability of their backs then they would be almost invincible, but one thing is sure and that is that Australia is going in the right direction and will be one of the top three or four sides in the World Cup in 1987.

9

The Best of Scottish

Without as yet having a divine right to the position, Heriot's FP have produced more than their fair share of full backs to the national side. It all began with Dan Drysdale who won 26 caps between 1923 and 1929, and was Scotland's full back throughout the Grand Slam season of 1925.

He was, of course, something of a legend, and as schoolboys we found it a hell of a lot easier to memorize the names and dates of the Heriot's full backs who had played for Scotland than to recite the dates and battles of the American Civil War. The tradition was carried on by Jimmy Kerr, Tommy Gray and Ian Thomson, and enjoyed one of its most dazzling periods during the reign of the incomparable Ken Scotland whose extreme modesty merely enhances his reputation as one of the greatest players to have graced the game.

I have often been compared to Kenny, probably because we were both essentially attacking players. It is generally recognized that Scotland was the forerunner of the modern full back. He turned the counterattack into something of an art form. His timing was impeccable, his footballing skills unrivalled.

He was succeeded by Colin Blaikie who was the Heriot's full back when I came into the side as a raw recruit on the wing, and was a source of great comfort and encouragement to me. After Colin came Ian Smith, in shape more like a prop than a full back but very much slower than your average prop! There can be no arguing with Smith's international record however – two tries in his first two internationals and had it not been for an injury against France in 1970/1 he might have won a few more caps.

I was the eighth in line and when I returned from the Lions tour to South Africa in 1974 it was decided to hold a dinner to honour the Heriot's full backs who had played for Scotland. It was a magnificent occasion, the first time that the eight of us had met. It reinforced my view that the purest pleasure in rugby comes not from Lions tours or from playing for one's country but from the involvement at grass roots level. The comradeship and spirit engendered by the club atmosphere is second to none, and for me the most enjoyable and exhilarating moments of my rugby career have been spent in the company of my friends at Goldenacre.

I have experienced more butterflies in the stomach in anticipation of a club game against Hawick or Gala than I ever did as captain of Scotland. Strangely, the responsibilities are far greater at club level where so much more is expected of the so-called star player. It was a responsibility I relished, especially during the years when the strength of the Heriot's side lay in the backs. We had to take risks to survive against the mighty Border backs of Hawick and Gala. I played alongside Fraser Dall, Harry Burnett and Jimmy Craig, a hugely talented midfield trio whose handling skills were on a par with the best of the Australians. In those days we lived and triumphed on 30 per cent possession.

In the first year of league rugby in Scotland, I vividly remember travelling to Mansfield Park to confront Hawick. Our cause appeared to be a hopeless one. We had taken some terrible beatings that season and Hawick were moving inexorably towards the first of their many league titles. But we ran everything and held them to an 18-all draw.

It is so much easier to foster team spirit within a club. On the Thursday night before a league encounter with one of the big guns we would be assured of a full turn-out. When Heriot's won the league title in 1979 we had perhaps five star players and six or seven donkeys. But invariably throughout that campaign we received better value from the donkeys than we did from the stars.

Until I became club captain and had to sit on the general committee I had no idea how much work was involved in the running of a club and how willingly busy men devoted their hard-earned free time to ensure that the operation ran smoothly. Players turn up twice weekly for training and on Saturdays for the game but have no concept of the work involved in making it all happen. The cleaning of the strips, the organization of the booze, the teas, the referee, the marking of the pitch. Someone has to sacrifice the time and effort and, as often as not, receives scant recognition from the players who tend to take it all for granted. Inevitably, they remember the one occasion when the bus fails to turn up rather than the countless times everything runs like clockwork.

I found it time-consuming enough to commit myself fully to the captaincy. There was little formalized coaching during my seasons as captain. I took the backs, ably assisted by Harry Burnett, Fraser Dall and Jimmy Craig, and later by Alan Lawson. Iain Milne, Jock Millican and David Robertson took charge of the forwards. As captain, I quite understood the outside pressures on first-team players. Absence from training for business or family reasons was quite acceptable but I would not tolerate lame excuses. Girl friends or bad weather left me unmoved and totally unsympathetic. If a player wanted to stay indoors watching television with his girl friend, I did not want him in my side.

I must confess to being something of a Corinthian in my attitude to the game. Winning is important of course. Were it not so, why would we bother to keep the score? But to me it has never been the be all and end all. In the first season of the Schweppes Leagues in Scotland, Heriot's won two matches and drew one of their last three games which was enough to keep us in the First division. But I reckon we had more fun out of that season than we did when we finished in mid-table in later years.

The celebrations after beating Langholm in 1974, where victory secured another year for us in the top league, were no less muted than they were when we defeated Haddington in 1979 to win the title for the first time.

We were fortunate in 1979 in that we caught Hawick cold at the start of that season and beat them at Goldenacre. Our sole defeat was against Gala. It was a tight game played in the Netherdale mud, and, with only about 30 per cent possession, we spent most of the time fighting a desperate rear guard action. I missed a couple of penalty kicks well within my compass which might have overturned the result but Gala deserved their 7–6 win. It was a surprisingly clean contest. I say surprisingly because there was much at stake and over the years I considered Gala to be the most physical – and at times brutal – side in Scotland.

It wasn't until we had beaten Boroughmuir, however, that outsiders gave us much chance of lifting the title and breaking the monopoly of Hawick and Gala. We had never performed well against Boroughmuir, especially at Meggetland. It had been an extremely hard winter but in the build-up to the fixture we had a massive turn-out at Goldenacre on training nights. Our training sessions were geared specifically to that one game with the result that we took the field fully briefed and highly motivated. I kicked off, and, with the adrenalin flowing a bit too freely, booted the ball directly into touch. At the scrum back on the half-way line I looked on in disbelief as Iain Milne and Jimmy Burnett lifted the entire Boroughmuir pack off the deck. From that moment, I knew that the game was ours for the taking. I also knew that there was nothing now to prevent us from winning the championship.

There have been better sides at Goldenacre than the one which took the title, but few more consistent. We were extremely fortunate with injuries and used no more than 18 players during the season. Ironically, I believe that we fielded our strongest side a couple of seasons after we had won the championship. Alan Lawson made a massive contribution at scrum half, as did David Robertson, who was possibly the biggest single influence in the side. A loose forward of astonishing pace, he was superbly fit and would certainly have been included in the Scottish party to tour New Zealand in 1981 and the party which went to Australia the following year had it not been for a bad ear injury. I look back fondly on the years of my captaincy of Heriot's as the most enjoyable period of my rugby career. And there is so much to savour.

My first taste of the big time was in 1972 when Heriot's played Cardiff at the Arms Park on the eve of the international between Scotland and Wales. Then, in the year of our title success, we went to Wembley and won the Charrington Festival, beating Rosslyn Park in the final. The next day we won the Harlequin Sevens at the Stoop Memorial Ground with a beautifully balanced team.

In winning the title in 1979 we had a remarkably well-balanced team. The front row was the best in Scotland with Callum Monro, a most underrated hooker, flanked by two international props in Iain Milne and Jimmy Burnett. We had two dedicated grafting locks in 'Dino' Stephen and Dougie Lynn. In the back row the indestructible Jock Millican was outstanding all season, and he was admirably supported by Hamish McDougall at number 8 and Peter O'Neill. Looking at our backs, as I have already mentioned, Dall, Harry Burnett and Craig were brilliant at club level. We were also very fortunate to have the fastest wing in Scottish rugby in Bill Gammell who was far and away our leading try scorer and, on the other wing, former Cambridge University Blue Steve Page was very quick and amazingly consistent. At scrum-half, Ian Duckworth was an extremely lively individual who was effective at launching our threequarters and was an equally good link with the pack.

At Heriot's, the backs have always been an influential part of a club whose basic philosophy has accommodated

120

and encouraged the cavalier approach that it matters not if a couple of tries are conceded so long as four are scored. It is an attitude shared in Scottish rugby by clubs like Watsonians and Stewarts-Melville.

In the early stages of my senior career I was greatly indebted to Lyn Tatham, a Leicestershire county player, who forced me to concentrate on my kicking and fielding. I wasn't very good at either, but he would voluntarily give two or three hours on a Wednesday afternoon to helping me improve. John Stent, who assisted with the coaching duties in our championship winning year, and Peter Hill, a physical education instructor who supervised the fitness training, also played an important part in my development both as a player and as an athlete. Hill's training schedules were carefully structured and designed to be both beneficial and fun. They were a major factor in our success in the 1978–79 season. It was at his insistence that every exercise contained a degree of competitiveness. There could be no shirking, no cheating.

This was in stark contrast to the subterfuges employed by some of the Lions during the 1977 tour in New Zealand. On the one hand, there were enthusiastic trainers like Ian McGeechan, J.J. Williams and myself and on the other skivers like John Bevan, later to be Welsh coach, who would stoop to every trick in the book to deceive John Dawes. The only ones they were deluding, of course, were themselves. But it annoyed me intensely. I believed that I had been given a certain amount of talent and that it was up to me to make the most of that talent. The very least I could do therefore was to keep myself fit. Again we were fortunate at Goldenacre in having enlightened administrators who would do everything in their power to provide us with the best and most up-to-date facilities. In my first year of captaincy our scrummaging machine was inadequate for our needs. At my insistence, however, and with the full backing of our President, David Edwards, the club purchased a new machine for £400 which turned out to be money well spent. We were equally well blessed when it came to matters of selection. Ken Scotland was chairman and knew the problems. If we did not perform particularly well one week, the committee resisted the temptation to make wholesale changes for the next game. There was a consistency of selection which made for stability and for consistency of performance on the field, and this contributed largely to our championship triumph in 1979.

Until recently, Heriot's have never possessed great strength in depth, but this has often worked to our advantage. Ian Duckworth, our scrum half in the 1978–9 season – his one and only season in the first XV – was due to attend his sister's wedding on the very day we were playing Hawick. Ian's decision to turn down the nuptial fixture for the Hawick game may well still rankle with his mother, but he played a vital role in our victory that day and scored a try. The next season Alan Lawson joined Heriot's and Duckworth lost his first XV place. But he nevertheless remained a loyal and valued member of the club for the next four or five years. Such loyalty, based on mutual respect and trust, is the very life-blood of club rugby and I will be eternally grateful to Heriot's for the fellowship I have experienced at Goldenacre.

The face of Scottish rugby altered radically with the establishment of the national leagues. They were roundly condemned by some at the beginning, and still have their critics, but they have the wholehearted support of the vast majority of players. Whether or not it has improved the performance at international level and had any substantial bearing on Scotland's Grand Slam in 1984 is a moot point, but it has undoubtedly given meaning to what was hitherto a shapeless domestic season, and has made the public at large very much more aware of the game in Scotland.

It is frequently the case nowadays that the largest crowds are to be found not at soccer grounds but at rugby grounds. Very few of the arguments put up against the leagues have proved to be valid. There has been no recognizable increase in violence, little evidence to suggest that games are any tighter in a league structure than they were under the old system. Heriot's may have had to give more thought to forward play than they did in the past but their basic principles have remained unaltered. Some of the most enjoyable, free-flowing games I have played in have been league games.

There are, however, two main areas of contention. The first concerns the number of clubs playing in the national leagues and the size of each league. In a country which has difficulty mustering a squad of 30 players capable of playing in international rugby, it seems absurd on the face of it to have a national league structure containing 98 clubs. In recent years several powerful voices have been raised in favour of reducing the numbers of clubs playing in the leagues and reducing the size of the leagues from 14 clubs, playing each other once a season in the league, to eight clubs playing on a home-and-away basis.

The system at present could still be improved, especially in the First Division where the gap between the top clubs and those at the bottom is well-nigh unbridgeable. With a few notable exceptions it is extremely hard for clubs promoted from the Second Division to remain in the First Division for more than one season, and some of the games are so one-sided that it is healthy neither for the victor nor for the vanquished. The classic example of this came a few seasons ago when Hawick and Gala were scoring more than 100 points against the same opposition on successive weeks. As it is, there are only half a dozen clubs at most who can offer serious resistance to Hawick and Gala.

There are strong arguments against the establishment of a premier league. The first is that it would create an elite which would foster disloyalty amongst those players of ambition playing for lesser clubs. Inevitably, the top clubs would be choosing from an enlarged pool of good players, while the clubs aspiring to higher things, having lost their star players, would have no opportunity to reach the upper echelons. These are perfectly valid arguments and one can sympathize with the smaller clubs for whom promotion to the First Division would be no more than a pipe dream. But they too would benefit from the experience gained by those players who had sampled life at the top when, in the fullness of time, they returned to the fold.

I have for long been a great admirer of the feeder system which operates so successfully at Hawick. The four junior clubs in that town have retained their own separate identities, but regard it as an honour to provide players to the full Hawick side just as Hawick are proud to be represented at national level. It may seem harsh on clubs like Hawick YM and Hawick Trades who could easily hold their own in the Second Division of the national leagues, but that is the way the system operates, and it is accepted and understood in that part of the country where the game is a religion. Apart from anything else, it is surely a damning indictment of the present league structure that junior sides like the Trades and YM could beat at least half of the so-called senior clubs lording it in the top 30.

The power base of the Scottish game is in the Borders, and despite the establishment of the national leagues the parochial nature of the Borderers is such that they tend to regard their own Border league, which has been in existence for longer than its national counterpart, as almost as important a competition. This attitude would surely change if the national leagues were reduced in size. The competition would be fierce, the best players would have the opportunity to test themselves each week in a more demanding environment, and with the competitive edge so much sharper it would soon manifest itself in the performance of the national XV. To illustrate my point, I would suggest that Jim Calder, had he been born and bred in Hawick, would be an even better player than he is at present. David Leslie was a marvellous player with Dundee High School FP and with West of Scotland, but it was only after he moved to Gala that he fulfilled his potential. Some years before, Nairn Mac-Ewan, the erstwhile Scottish coach, travelled thousands of miles during a season from his home in Inverness to play each week for Gala and was rewarded with a place in the Scottish side. It is only natural for a talented player to seek to discover the top limits of his ability, and with all deference to these players, and in the certain knowledge that the standard of rugby in Scotland would improve, I consider it important to make changes to the national league structure.

The second area of contention concerns the refusal to allow replacements in league matches. I consider this ludicrous and positively dangerous. We have the best-organized league system in the country, far ahead of its kind and still in advance of anything in existence in England and Wales, and yet the archaic and outdated arguments which are dusted down and brought out at the annual meeting of the Scottish clubs still manage to carry the day. There have been many occasions when I have stayed on the field with sundry injuries rather than leave my team-mates short-handed. It is positively barbaric and insane and I am confident that my view is shared by almost 100 per cent of the players.

The principal argument against replacements is that rugby is a game to be played and that by allowing replacements you are denying a chap the chance of participating in the sport. What is often forgotten is that a player would probably much rather be given the chance of appearing briefly in the first XV rather than playing for 80 minutes in the seconds. No one is suggesting for a minute that there should be the same replacements each week. It could, and should, be done on a rota basis. If players are being asked to play competitively within a league structure where points are at stake, and where there are financial implications for the club in victory and defeat, it is only right and proper that the rules of that competition should be seen to be just. I have not the slightest doubt that Gala would have won the league title in the 1981–2 season had they beaten us. That they didn't was largely due to the fact that they played for all but five minutes of the game without David Leslie who broke his leg. Even against 14 men we struggled to win, and only did so by the narrowest of margins, but that defeat cost Gala the championship.

The concentration of talent in the Borders has obviously had its effect not only on the club scene in Scotland but also at district level. The inter-district championship has, except for brief spells of token resistance by Glasgow and Edinburgh, been dominated by the South. In the early 1970s, when I first started playing representative rugby, Glasgow had as fine a collection of forwards as they have ever possessed in Ian McLauchlan, Quintin Dunlop, Sandy Carmichael and Gordon Brown, and thanks to them they succeeded in wresting the initiative from the South – though invariably when they played Edinburgh their shortcomings in the backs would be highlighted and, despite losing the tight-head count sometimes 10–0, we would still manage to sneak a win. But the pendulum has swung back in favour of the South and seems certain to remain there for some time to come.

The introduction of the Anglo-Scots to the district championship in recent years has given the competition more variety and has added to its stature, but there is still a marked imbalance, and in my view the Scottish districts would benefit greatly from some cross-border fraternization. They should expand their horizons and should play more often against top English counties such as Lancashire and Gloucestershire and the leading Welsh sides like Llanelli, Cardiff and Swansea.

It should never be forgotten that we are a tiny rugby-playing community and do extraordinarily well with our limited resources, but we can always improve. Whenever possible we should be seeking to raise our standards by measuring ourselves against the best available opposition. We are able to survive at international level and, once in a blue moon as happened in 1984, lead the parade, but in the main we have in Jim Telfer's words 'to run very hard just to stand still'. We can put 15 players onto the international field who are capable of holding their own and at a stretch could perhaps find another six. But were we to pit our third XV against the equivalent from England, Wales or France I have no doubt that we would be annihilated. Great credit therefore is due to those in Scotland who have succeeded in making a little go a long way. Very often we have managed to make a silk purse out of a sow's ear but equally the country has miraculously produced more than its fair share of silk purses. I would like to mention some of them.

When I first came into the Scottish side the strength lay in the 'Famous Five' tight forwards – McLauchlan, Madsen, Carmichael, Gordon Brown and McHarg – and there can be no doubt that few countries have been able to field a more formidable unit. McLauchlan was easily the outstanding loose head in my experience. As a captain he was extremely demanding, although we were never quite on the same wavelength in our attitudes towards the game. His team talks were nothing short of brutal but he was an uncommonly skilful motivator. There could be no doubt that he had the respect of his forwards. They recognized that although he was ready to call the tune on occasions he was also prepared to take punishment and probably received more than his fair share of stick over the years for his trouble.

There have been two exceptionally fine Scottish hookers during my international career – Duncan Madsen and Colin Deans. Madsen was physically more robust but lacked the aggression of Deans and could not begin to compete with him as a footballer. Had Deans been a stone heavier he would have been in a class apart. But what he lacks in physique Deans has more than compensated for with his pace, courage and dedication. A magnificent all-round forward.

There is a very delicate decision to be made at tight head. Sandy Carmichael or my club colleague Iain Milne? Carmichael's value to his side tended to be underestimated. He went on two Lions tours and was good enough to have played in eight Tests. But he didn't play in any. If he had a fault, and it can hardly be described as that, it was that he was perhaps too much of a gentleman. Carmichael was an immensely strong man, utterly free of malice. He would never use his strength to intimidate or maltreat opponents weaker or less skilful than himself. But it is a fact of life that to succeed at the very top in the twilight world of front-row play, a degree of meaness is essential. Carmichael had everything – power, speed, technique and he was a devastating tackler. I still shudder when I recall one particular cover tackle he made on the English centre David Cooke. But he lacked the cold, calculating mind which would have elevated him to legendary status.

Iain Milne is altogether a much more aggressive type. Not in Carmichael's class in the loose but unquestionably the cornerstone of Scotland's Grand Slam pack. Milne's physique would also be important if I were to have McLauchlan and Deans as the other members of my front row triumvirate. 'The Bear', as he is nicknamed, weighs 17½ stone, and although he lacked Carmichael's pace in the loose, Milne is deceptively fast for one of his bulk. I would therefore give my vote to Milne but it would be by the shortest of neck muscles!

Gordon Brown is out on his own as my first choice lock. He played in eight Lions Tests which would have been ten had he remained free of injury. Sadly for Scotland, Brown always reserved his best performances for the Lions and personally I always felt sorry that the Scottish supporters never saw the best of this great forward. However, in common with most men of his size, Brown was never at peak fitness during the domestic season and it was only when he was subjected to the daily rigours of training on a major tour that he blossomed into a top-class forward. Had I had any say in the matter I would have personally supervised Brown's training schedules during the home international series. He was a natural footballer which cannot often be said about second-row forwards. His career, as I explain in greater detail later in the book, was blighted by the incident in the inter-district match in 1977 when he was involved in a fracas with Allan Hardie, the North Midlands hooker, and was sent off. His retaliation was a major offence for which he deserved to be punished, but he was unfortunate that the incident coincided with the SRU's campaign to clean up the game. Brown, unlike a number of other international players, was not one of the lunatic fringe who take a psychopathic delight in maiming opponents. He was a hard man, of course, and quite able to defend himself, but he was not a dirty player. It was sad for Brown and sad for Scotland, who had to play throughout that season without their best forward.

Brown's regular partner in the Scottish second row was the unorthodox and undeniably eccentric Alastair McHarg, the best middle of the line jumper that I have ever seen and the best auxiliary full back I've ever played with. He was also one of the finest loose forwards and a centre three-quarter of no mean ability. And it was his totally unconventional approach to tight forward play which was his weakness, although there were never any complaints about his ability to scrummage. But there was an understandable suspicion amongst selectors and critics that any lock who got about the field with McHarg's sprightliness could not be doing his full share in the tight, and if I had to choose a second row to fit in alongside Brown, I would probably plump for Alan Tomes. They locked the Scottish scrum together in 1976 when we beat England at Murrayfield and Ireland at Lansdowne Road. McHarg, if memory serves me right, played number 8 in those two matches.

Just as Brown would be an automatic choice for the second row in my Scottish select XV, so David Leslie would be the first name down in the back row. Despite the fact that he has played number 8 and considers it to be his best position, I would play him as an open-side flanker. He is a player of true world class, whose failure to make a Lions tour is a travesty. Injury was partly responsible for his omission in 1980, but his absence from the 1983 tour to New Zealand was rank bad selection in my view. Leslie is a Jekyll and Hyde character. He is articulate and intelligent, and off the field a gentleman who would be the first to help an old lady across the road. But when the whistle goes all hell is let loose. He is a thinking man's player, someone with a good brain and tremendous insight. Furthermore, he is a superb footballer as befits one who, as a schoolboy, played at stand off. But it is his fearlessness bordering on the reckless which lifts him above the ordinary. His driving technique is in the finest traditions of New Zealand forward play, his tackling lethally accurate. His agility makes up for a lack of the height at the line-out and had he been a more enthusiastic trainer there is no knowing what he could have achieved. Unfortunately, if any criticism was to be levelled at Leslie it was that he was not always the most dedicated of trainers. I imagine his argument would have been that he did not want to leave his best work on the training ground. Although he won the total respect of everyone on the field I know of several players who were less than amused by his antics in training. The result was that he tended to play in bursts and perhaps lacked the stamina of a Slattery or a Rives who could run for the full 80 minutes.

For all that he was the man I would happily follow into the jungle, and very probably the man I would choose to lead my side. I never played under Leslie as a captain, but his courage, intelligence and all-round skill make him ideally qualified for the job. He also had the advantage of playing in the back row, up with the forwards but in touch with the backs, and therefore well placed to lead.

On the other flank, five players spring to mind – Jim Calder, Jock Millican, Mike Biggar, Gordon Strachan and Nairn McEwan. Calder, like Leslie, was a fine ball player, and one of the most constructive flank forwards to have played for Scotland. He was brought into the Scottish side to tighten up the defence on the left side of the scrummage, and did a remarkably effective job. He may have lacked Leslie's aggression but was generally fitter and gave 100 per cent effort for the full 80 minutes.

Millican's international career was cut short by injury which was a great loss because, to my mind, Millican was a player in the Rives and Slattery mould. He did not possess a quarter of their finesse with the ball in his hands but there can have been few faster men about the field and few deadlier in the tackle. Strachan was never given the recognition his talent deserved. He was versatile enough to play in all three back-row positions, and was a member of a successful Scottish side, but, unaccountably, he fell out of favour after a mediocre showing against the Argentinians. In Mike Biggar, Scotland was well served for a number of seasons by a real, genuine, grafting stalwart.

Scotland have been fortunate in having a choice of two first-class number 8s in recent years. There has been a battle royal between John Beattie and Iain Paxton with the latter having enjoyed the better of the exchanges. Beattie was unfortunate in that his career was cruelly interrupted by a serious knee injury, but for my money he has always looked a player capable of reaching the heights. He is a superb physical specimen. He possesses aggression, a hint of meanness and explosive pace. In his first full season of international rugby in 1980 he was selected for the Lions, and it was unfortunate that the tour management on that occasion allowed him to drift through the tour and to seek his own salvation rather than offer him advice and encouragement to bring the best out of him. He could have been an enormous asset on that tour and should have returned home a much more mature player. I doubt that he has ever quite recovered from the knee injury he received in 1981.

Iain Paxton, to give him credit, took his chance and it was interesting to see that it was Paxton who emerged as first choice for the 1983 Lions in the Test series against the All Blacks. P.C. Brown was another candidate and without doubt the best line-out man of the three. But Brown was basically a lock forward playing as a number 8 and lacked the pace so necessary nowadays.

Three scrum halfs have spanned my period of occupancy in the Scottish side and all three – Alan Lawson, Douglas Morgan and Roy Laidlaw – have possessed outstanding qualities. At one end of the scale is Lawson – alert, lethally swift over the first 20 yards, and a creator of chances *par excellence* with as long and as smooth a pass as any stand off could wish for. Alan was not perhaps the best defensive player in the world, but having played several seasons with him in the Heriot's side, I can categorically say he was an (absolute) joy to play with each week.

At the other end of the scale was Douglas Morgan. Gritty, determined and pugnacious – a forward's dream but lacking Lawsons's vision and flair for attack. Occupying the centre ground is Roy Laidlow. Defensively sound, fearless and equally at home in the cloying mud of New Zealand or on the baked surface of the South African high veldt. He seldom scorned an opportunity to break and scored a host of tries on the blind side, his two in the Triple Crown winning match at Lansdowne Road in 1984 being classic examples.

In contrast to the scrum-half position there is only one stand off who comes into the frame – John Rutherford. Not having played with the likes of Gordon Waddell or Angus Cameron and playing only briefly with Colin Telfer, when he was past his prime but was nevertheless one of the finest kickers of the ball I have seen, I would imagine that you would have to go back to the Wilson Shaw era to find a player capable of matching John Rutherford. Of the stand offs in my time Phil Bennett would be the only player of comparable class. Early on in John's international career he had no inhibitions. He played the game instinctively and his instinct was to attack. Some of our happiest times in the Scottish sides were when we decided to run everything and, with runners of the calibre of Rutherford, Renwick and Keith Robertson, we had considerable fire power.

Unlike Bennett who tended to dart through gaps like a startled rabbit, Rutherford was more elegant in his running, using all the subtlety of pace to beat opponents. I consider that Rutherford would have made a first-class job of captaining his country and still might do so. He is a masterly reader of a game and is in the best possible position at stand off to call the shots.

The pairing in the centre is ready-made – Jim Renwick and Ian McGeechan, both masters of their particular craft. Renwick possessed one of the sharpest minds in rugby. A beautifully balanced runner he could create something out of nothing. To me, he is the complete player whose influence in the game would have been much greater had the Lions selectors possessed a fraction of his rugby brain and had picked him earlier on in his career. As it was, they overlooked him for the 1977 tour to New Zealand and granted him only one Test in South Africa in 1980.

McGeechan was the most unselfish of players and, as a result, his own contribution was often underrated. Like Renwick, he was quick, tenacious and positive in everything that he did. They were a perfect blend. McGeechan reserved, but possessing a Yorkshireman's good sense and dry humour, and Renwick with his biting wit was always chirpy and great fun. He and I were very similar in our approach and attitudes to the game. We enjoyed a great mutual respect and understanding, which was why I so enjoyed playing in the same back-line with him.

Without having anyone of the class of Gerald Davies, David Duckham or Grant Batty for the wing positions, Scotland has fielded some highly talented players throughout the 1970s and into the 1980s. There would be very little separating Billy Steele and Keith Robertson. Steele was the better attacking player, swifter than Robertson, but lacking the Melrose man's defensive solidity. Robertson, to my mind, is the complete footballer who is equally at home on the wing or in the centre, and I have a personal hunch that he would have made an excellent full back. The other outstanding three quarter has been David Johnston. He has tremendous pace, and, for a small man, he is a tenacious defender.

Roger Baird suffered a loss of form during Scotland's Grand Slam season but who can ever forget his electrifying burst which opened the flood-gates in the game against Wales at Cardiff in 1982? Potentially the best wing we have had in my time, I would like to see Roger adopt a hungrier attitude in his search for the ball. He has everything else, and I think his best is yet to come.

David Shedden, the West of Scotland wing, was pound for pound the best tackler I have seen. We nicknamed him 'Rattling Bones' but inside that spare frame, which weighed no more than 9½ stone, beat the heart of a tiger. And then there was Bruce Hay whose lack of pace never appeared to be a handicap for the simple reason that Hay was one of the fortunate few whose experience enabled him to do the right thing at the right time. He was an opportunist with the priceless gift of being able to score tries. He was also a marvellously comforting player to have as an auxiliary full back.

There were times, when the weather was wet and the ball heavy, when I thought it would have been prudent to switch Bruce to full back and to move me to the wing. But for my dream team I would of course require perfect conditions and would unhesitatingly pick myself at full back! My team – Irvine; Robertson, McGeechan, Renwick, Baird; Rutherford, Laidlaw; McLauchlan, Deans, Milne, Tomes, Brown, Leslie, Calder and Paxton.

A team of such varied talents would very probably be able to operate on auto-pilot, but I would have Jim Telfer as coach. Bill Dickinson, the first man to be appointed national coach, although he was then designated as advisor to the captain, did a splendid job in improving Scottish forward play and building the solid forward base from which Scotland launched her offensives well into the 1970s. But Bill rarely addressed himself to the backs. Telfer has also been criticized for concentrating too much of his efforts on the forwards and being too narrow in his approach to the game. That may certainly have been true in the early part of his career when he was still under the influence of a Melrose side in which there were eight good forwards plus Hastie and Chisholm at half-back. But although Jim lost none of his passion for developing forward play, or his dedication to fitness and meticulous preparation, his attitude towards backs changed and he became a much better coach as a result. There is absolutely no doubt that he had more to do with Scotland's Grand Slam than any other individual. To me he epitomizes all that is good in Scottish rugby.

10

To South Africa in 1974

A business engagement in Arbroath meant that I had to leave Edinburgh before the post arrived, and the first news I received of my selection for the Lions party to tour South Africa was on the car radio. I'd had an inkling that I would be selected. Norman Mair, the *Scotsman* rugby correspondent, had telephoned the previous night to say that he had heard a whisper from Carwyn James, so I was fairly optimistic.

Scotland had had a reasonable season, beating England and France and losing by just three points to Ireland, the eventual champions. Our forwards had played superbly against the Irish; we beat England with my last minute penalty goal after David Duckham had run off-side, and we gave our best team performance in the final match of the season against France. I was desperately keen to go. When I was first selected for Scotland as a 21-year-old I felt at the time that all my ambitions had been fulfilled, but now, with two seasons in the international side behind me, I aspired to higher things.

At that point it was enough that I had been selected for the Lions. J. P. R. Williams was obviously going as the number one full-back, and as he was well nigh indestructible I knew that it would be very difficult to oust him from the Test side. I must confess that I did not greatly concern myself with the make-up of the rest of the party. I was interested, of course, especially in the Scottish players, but the criticisms of the selection washed over me. The chief surprise seemed to be the omission of John Pullin who had captained England on their successful tour to South Africa in 1972 and who had been the Lions Test hooker in New Zealand in 1971.

On later tours I suppose I took a keener interest in selection but on this occasion I was so darned glad to be a part of it that I had no wish to become emotionally involved in the sins of omission or commission of the selectors. In retrospect I believe it was the best selection of any of the Lions tours in which I took part. I think they got it just about right in every position although I would certainly have picked Jim Renwick. Seeing the team in black and white in the newspapers the next day was much like reading a roll of honour – Willie John McBride as the captain, Gareth Edwards, Mervyn Davies, Mike Gibson and Phil Bennett. The tour party was to be managed by Alun Thomas of Wales, and the coach was Syd Millar of Ireland.

The real fascination for me lay in the fact that I had never previously toured abroad. I'd read tour books and heard tour stories of the 1971 trip to New Zealand which had whetted my appetite. Now I was going to experience the twin delights of touring South Africa and of wearing a Lions jersey. I can remember vividly arriving at Heathrow Airport and seeing an enormous hulk of metal – my first sighting of a jumbo jet. My wide-eyed amazement and uncontrollable excitement were almost childlike. Even the administrative chores were a pleasure. We had to sign documents to the effect that we would abide by the laws of the country we were touring, and that we would maintain a certain standard of behaviour.

Our pocket money allowance was 50 pence a day. A lot has been written and said about the parsimony of the four home unions, unfairly in my opinion. It is, after all, an allowance to cover incidental expenses, postcards, letters and suchlike. The Lions are royally entertained on tour. Generally speaking no expense is spared to ensure that the players have everything they need. To my knowledge no player ever went short of food or drink on a

137

tour, and when you add it up over a 12-week period, 50 pence a day went a long way in those days.

We arrived at Johannesburg at the ungodly hour of seven in the morning and to our astonishment discovered a welcoming party of about 3,000. From Johannesburg we were taken by bus some 40 miles out of the city to Stilfontein. The accommodation was modest by comparison with what was to follow but, in my rose-tinted view, was palatial. There were swimming pools, playing fields and training facilities. What more could a fit young athlete want?

I have always enjoyed training and therefore revelled in Syd Millar's fitness sessions which were brutally hard and all the more punishing in the early stages because we were operating at 5,000 feet above sea level. I had been transplanted to a different world of long sunny days, daily training in the morning, golf, tennis or swimming in the afternoons, usually in the company of Dick Milliken, the Irish centre, and my compatriot Ian McGeechan. It was our first taste of touring and for all three of us it was paradise. The warmth and friendship of our hosts was quite unbelievable. Nothing was too much trouble for them. I remember that on the morning of the game against Northern Transvaal in Pretoria I went to Johannesburg to collect some diamonds that I had bought earlier in the tour. Unfortunately, time ran against me and it was clear that I was going to be late for the team talk. I explained my predicament to the diamond merchant who immediately telephoned the police. Minutes later two patrol cars arrived and with sirens blaring, I was chauffeured at an average speed of 95 miles an hour to our hotel in Pretoria.

Socially, the 1974 tour was the best in my experience. Syd Millar was a stern taskmaster on the training field, but he knew when to call a halt and when to allow the players to relax. He encouraged us to get out and meet the locals, which is much easier in South Africa where the sun invariably shines, than it is in New Zealand where, as often as not, it is raining and the touring parties tend to become bored and introverted.

We were richly blessed with characters. Mickey Burton was a superb mimic and raconteur, Billy Steele an inspiring choirmaster and Bobby Windsor possessed a wit as sharp as it was mischievous. His finest moment came at the expense of Alun Thomas. There is a strict rule concerning the charging of private telephone bills to the collective account. In short you can't. On one occasion the manager was handed a telephone bill for £87.00 which had been charged to his room. He was furious and called a meeting of the players in order to unmask the culprit. 'All right lads', he said, 'has anyone got the decency to own up to this appalling deceit?' Silence. 'That being the case', continued Thomas with a disturbing air of confidence, 'I must expose the culprit myself. I have checked with the International Operator and the calls were made to Newport 684210'. At which point an outraged Windsor leapt to his feet. 'OK you bastards,' he screamed, 'which one of you has been phoning my wife!' The entire gathering collapsed with laughter and Thomas, totally disarmed, did the only decent thing – he paid the bill himself.

There can be few better places to tour in the world than South Africa. The weather is marvellous and there are so many pleasing ways of passing the time. One treasured memory for me in 1974 was the visit to the Kruger Game Park. As members of the Lions, we were privileged guests and went with the rangers to areas banned from the general public. Those crisp clear nights under the stars and the magnificent barbecues in the Kruger Park are imperishable memories and are as much part of touring as playing rugby. It was quite incomprehensible to me that some of the players never left the compound, choosing instead to spend their days boozing in the midst of such splendour.

On the other hand, you can be too adventurous as I found out to my cost in Durban. We were playing football on the beach when one of the forward donkeys

139

hoofed the ball into the water. I obligingly dived in to retrieve it but was carried out and swept onto some rocks. The coastguard had to swim to my aid because my feet had been lacerated on the coral reef. I had resolved before the tour began that I would take full advantage of the opportunities that presented themselves. Had I wanted to booze I could just as easily have done so at home. Consequently, I saw as much as I could of South Africa and was enchanted by the magnificence of Rhodesia.

I also made a point of getting to know the local people. It is all too easy to brand them as 'heavies', thereby relieving yourself of your responsibility as a rugby tourist. Admittedly, there are times when the socializing becomes tedious but I know from my own experience how enjoyable it can be to talk with people who have a specialized knowledge of a subject. I have met Jack Nicklaus on a couple of occasions and have been fascinated to hear his thoughts on golf. How does he rate Augusta? Is it more of a test than Muirfield? I take the view that as an international sportsman I have a duty to impart whatever knowledge I have about the game to those who are genuinely interested in hearing about it. Paradoxically, the social success of a tour at this level depends on the success of the team on the field and our experiences in South Africa in 1974 were all the better for the fact that we kept winning our matches.

It was understandable that one or two of the players should have been disappointed at not making the Test side, and this may have affected their attitude towards the country and to the tour as a whole. But I had made up my mind that, come what may, I would make the most of every opportunity. I resolved to train as hard as I could and hoped that eventually I would be selected for a Test match either at full back – in the unlikely event of J. P. R. being injured – or on the wing.

Syd Millar gave me every encouragement. He was something of a father figure to me. To be perfectly frank I don't think that he was a great coach, but then our requirement on that tour was not so much for a coach as for someone with intelligence, organizational skill and an understanding of man management. Millar possessed all these qualities in abundance. He knew that there was nothing he could teach Gareth Edwards or Phil Bennett. They controlled the game. Bennett ran when he liked and kicked when the occasion demanded it, whilst Edwards was light years ahead of anything the Springboks could put out against him. I don't think I have ever seen a player with so much confidence.

Millar gave us our freedom but when he asked for discipline he got it. Such was the respect that the players had for him. For the first three or four weeks of the tour I was having terrible problems catching the high ball. So, what's new, you ask? Believe me, I was particularly fallible out there because of the sun and the thin atmosphere. Syd knew that I was upset by it and set about repairing my confidence. He organized special clinics after training during which Ian McGeechan, Phil Bennett and Alan Old would pump high balls at me. After a couple of weeks there was a definite improvement.

Millar was criticized as being too inflexible and for failing to get the best out of the backs. It is true that his attitude may have been conditioned by his experiences in South Africa as a player in 1962 and again in 1968. He believed that you could not beat the Springboks without a competitive scrummage and in 1974 he had, in his Test and shadow packs, two superb packs. In that context I believe that the art of coaching is really the art of organizing. Millar was fortunate in that he had some of the best British forwards of all time – Franny Cotton, Gordon Brown, Fergus Slattery and Mervyn Davies – the latter pair being, I believe, the key players in the Lions success. Slattery's speed over the ground was invaluable and it was one of the failings of succeeding Lions tours that they did not possess a player of Slattery's pace and commitment in the back row. The 1974 Lions were so talented that no matter who had been coach or captain it would have been successful.

141

Take the captaincy for instance. If it hadn't been given to Willie John there were plenty of other candidates. There were eleven members in the party who had either already captained their countries or who would do so in future years. McBride was described as being a great captain. He was undoubtedly a good captain but not a great one. He had many outstanding qualities. He was a legendary figure, a first class motivator and an excellent after-dinner speaker, but on the field, although he and Ian McLauchlan ran the show up front, I felt that it was Bennett and Edwards who controlled the team. McBride's chief advantage was that he was older and wiser than the rest of us. But from the tactical point of view, as I'm sure McBride himself would be the first to agree, he didn't have much influence.

Windhoek is not perhaps the most picturesque part of South Africa. Lying closer to the equator than most of the country it is very hot, very dry and the ground has a rock-like quality detested by touring full backs. But Windhoek will always have a special place in my affections for it was there that I wore the Lions jersey for the first time. I did not play particularly well. The bounce of the ball deceived me on a number of occasions and the mighty Jan Ellis, the former Springbok captain and the local hero, was much too full of running for my liking. It was a game we were never going to lose but one we laboured to win.

Thereafter we advanced with varying degrees of comfort through the next six games in the build-up to the First Test, my only claim to fame being that in our 97–0 rout of South West District I failed to score a single point. The game served no useful purpose. There was no great satisfaction in being on the winning side and less, I should imagine, in being on the losing one. It was no help to the Lions selectors who were by this time anxious to find the best possible Test combination.

The selection of the side for the next game, against Western Province at Newlands, the venue for the First Test on the following Saturday, was the most significant of the tour to date. J.P.R. was at full back, Clive Rees and Billy Steele were on the wing, and, rather surprisingly, Tony Neary, Stewart McKinney and Andy Ripley were in the back row. The Lions won 17–8 without looking totally convincing, and several of the party who had watched the game from the stand believed that there were still places to be won in the Test side.

For the midweek game against the Proteas (The Cape Coloureds) the back-row forwards were Roger Uttley, Fergus Slattery and Mervyn Davies. J.J. Williams was on the left wing and Fran Cotton was at tight head prop. It was an extraordinary game. The Proteas were total strangers to the laws and were kami-kazi tacklers into the bargain – a lethal combination. Alan Old had been on the bench when England had played the Proteas two years previously, and had thanked his lucky stars that he wasn't playing on that occasion. The opposition had taken the field with the sole purpose of keeping the score down and had not been the least bit fussy about how they achieved their aims. The memory had left its mark on Alan who knew that he was still very much in contention for the Test side. He did not relish the encounter, and as it turned out his sense of foreboding was fully justified. He was so badly injured by a horrifically late tackle in the first half that one of his knee ligaments was severed. His leg was put in plaster and three weeks later he returned home.

But one member of the opposition did impress me that day. He saw very little of the ball but on the few occasions that he was given space he moved like a thoroughbred. He was young and extremely raw. But his talent shone through. His name was Errol Tobias. The problems we encountered on the field against the Proteas were balanced by the fact that we were the first Lions side to have played against a coloured team. We were all very conscious of the anti-apartheid feeling in Britain and elsewhere. We knew the arguments for and against the tour but I have to admit that although I was upset by some of the things I saw on that 1974 visit, I was so

143

thrilled to be a part of it that I didn't give the political problems of South Africa much thought. I went out of my way to speak to the Proteas players after the match and immediately struck up a friendship with Tobias with whom I played in the same Presidents XV against England at Twickenham ten years later. That friendship and camaraderie which unites people is surely the single most important argument in favour of maintaining sporting links with South Africa or with any other country whose political views do not happen to coincide with your own.

Despite the fact that I was not in the side for the First Test it was impossible not to be affected by the tension and a certain amount of apprehension. Although we had reached this stage of the tour unbeaten and had built up enormous understanding and large reserves of confidence, we were still an unknown quantity in Test terms. So, of course, were the Springboks. The South African selectors had chosen to ignore the evidence of their own trial and had allowed themselves to be influenced by the Western Province display against the Lions the previous Saturday. Seven of their players were selected, including Roy McCallum, the scrum half, who had not even played in the trial.

The Lions decided that Fran Cotton, who had originally been selected as a loose head, should play on the tight head in place of Sandy Carmichael. The Scot had been prevented by injury from playing in a Test match in New Zealand in 1971, and he was therefore to gain the unenviable distinction of going on two Lions tours without playing in a Test. It was hard luck on a very fine player. But Gordon Brown won the lock position beside Willie John, Mighty Mouse McLauchlan was at loose head, and Billy Steele and the ever-reliable Ian McGeechan were the Scots in the back division. It was also decided that Roger Uttley would do the same job for us in South Africa that Derek Quinnell had done so effectively for the 1971 Lions in New Zealand. It was a wise decision.

Sitting in the stand it very soon became clear that the Lions were comfortably on top in the scrummage. The conditions were unpleasant – the pitch was heavy and there was a strong wind blowing down field. But Edwards began to dominate the play with those mischievously placed kicks of his which skidded on the greasy surface and kept the pressure on the Springboks defence. With the wind behind them the Springboks had been unable to conjure anything more than a drop goal from the first half. They must have smelt a defeat just as the Lions sensed victory. With our forwards firmly in control Phil Bennett kicked three penalties and Gareth Edwards dropped a goal. The one-sidedness of the contest was best summed up by Doctor Danie Craven, the venerable President of the South African Rugby Board who, in accordance with Springbok tradition, was presenting the newly capped players with their caps and blazers. 'I have to make this presentation to Chris Pope', said the good Doctor, 'who has created something of a record by becoming the first Springbok to play for his country without touching the ball.' Pope had spent a lonely day on the wing.

Those who thought that the First Test was one-way traffic should have been at Pretoria for the second international a fortnight later. The Lions scored five tries and trounced their demoralized opponents 28–9. It was getting progressively more difficult to see a way into this side, but the week before the Third Test I was selected on the wing against Northern Transvaal and when the side was announced for the Port Elizabeth Test I was in on the right wing in place of Billy Steele.

I was enough of a realist to know that I owed my selection more to the fact that there was some doubt about Phil Bennett's fitness and that I might be required as a goal kicker, rather than to my abilities as a winger. Billy Steele was an experienced wing, more familiar with defensive alignment than I was. I would have been much happier at full back where I had a lot more to contribute, but I was tickled pink to be in the side and to be involved in the build-up which was the most intensive that I have ever experienced. From a personal point of view the game was hardly memorable. I saw very little of the ball. I made a couple of tackles, kicked two penalties (one very satisfyingly from 70 yards) and a conversion, and that was the sum total of my involvement.

But I do recall that they came at us like bats out of hell in the first quarter. Their pride and honour were at stake. They were two down in the series and had been pilloried by their own press. They picked out J.P.R. as the target of their opening assault. Twice he unflinchingly took high balls together with half the Springbok pack and I just thought, 'Jesus Christ, rather him than me!' It was a bruising contest during which the infamous '99' call, when all the Lions would immediately rush to the aid of a colleague in trouble, was sounded on several occasions. Fights broke out at regular intervals, and in one of them Gordon Brown broke his hand. My role in all this mayhem was that of passive bystander.

It wasn't until I reached the sanctuary of the dressing room that I realized the full significance of our achievement. We had won the match 26–9 and with it the series – the first Lions side to do so in South Africa. It was the first real sense of satisfaction that I had experienced on the tour. The celebrations lasted far into the night and the following morning. The Lions had now established beyond all reasonable doubt that they were vastly superior to the Springboks. All that remained was to win the remaining provincial matches and complete the whitewash in the Test series.

In the lead-up to the final Test we beat Border, Natal and Eastern Transvaal with something to spare although the game against Natal was marred by the altercation between J.P.R. and Tommy Bedford, which ended up with blows being exchanged. It was a distasteful incident and unworthy of the two great players involved.

The entire population of Johannesburg, it seemed, turned up at Ellis Park for the Fourth Test. There wasn't an inch of space. Spectators were draped over the scaffolding and every possible vantage point was occupied. We knew that the Springboks would be more determined than ever. There would be no hiding place for those who had lost all four Tests in a home series. The Lions on the other hand were naturally easing off as thoughts were increasingly turning towards home. Furthermore, McGeechan, Bennett, Milliken and Windsor had been troubled by a stomach bug and although all four were passed fit to play there was no telling how weakened they had been by the virus.

The match was only a few minutes old when Windsor was in the wars and played out the remainder of the game with a severe head wound and, very possibly, concussion. Nevertheless we took the lead when Roger Uttley beat Pope to the touchdown. Then, a typical piece of Edwards magic gave me a clear run for our second try. Bennett had converted Uttley's try but was clearly out of touch with his place kicking, a misfortune which led to the most testing moment of my tour.

The Springboks worked hard to repair the early damage and in the closing minutes of the first half they kicked a penalty. They came at us with renewed intensity in the second half. Their scrummage was more comfortable than at any other time during the series. Cronje scored a try, the Springboks first of the series, and Snyman gave them a 13–10 lead with another penalty. It was the first time that the Lions had looked vulnerable. With five minutes left we were awarded a penalty which was none the easier for the fact that it was in a relatively simple position – less than 25 yards out and half-way in from touch. Bennett was not exactly begging to take the kick so the responsibility fell on me. The moment I struck the ball I instinctively knew that the contact had not been clean. The ball squeezed in at the left hand post but so tight was it that neither touch judge seemed certain. That kick more than anything else brought home to me the pressures of playing Test rugby. 13–13 as the most controversial moment of the tour approached. Slattery drove for the Springboks' line and appeared to get the touchdown for the try which would have won the game but Max Baise, the referee, ordered a five-yard scrummage. There were various emotions in the changing room afterwards – anger, disgust and everywhere a sense of anti-climax.

Nevertheless it had been a magnificent tour. Alun Thomas has described the 1974 team as 'the greatest Lions in history' and very few of us sitting in the Ellis Park changing room after the final Test would have subscribed to John Reason's view that not only had we failed to live up to our potential but that we had sowed the seeds of the stultifying back play which was to characterize British and Irish rugby in later years.

Syd Millar believed from first to last that the Test series would be won in the scrummage and whereas the brilliant Lions backs of 1971 had to take every chance offered to them, the 1974 side were so dominant that they could afford the luxury of playing the game in their opponent's half. They could even afford to be profligate on occasions although the plan was to keep mistakes to a minimum. J. P. R. mostly played the orthodox full back's role while Gareth Edwards and Phil Bennett kicked a great deal from half-back. The strength of the side undoubtedly lay in the forwards so there seemed a great deal of logic in Millar's philosophy. Personally, I derived most enjoyment from the midweek matches where we could take risks. We had as much possession as we wanted, ran to our hearts content and scored tries by the dozen.

But so inferior was the opposition that any reasonable club side in Britain would have beaten them. As for the Test series it was also undeniably true that we caught the Springboks unprepared. They had been starved of international competition for four years. Even by the end of the tour they had failed to find their best side. In the first three Tests they used 32 players; they came nowhere near matching the Lions in the scrummage and for once they did not possess an effective back-row unit. They were in a quandary about their half-back pairing and for

148

the first Test, which was played in conditions most foul, they picked a running side. By contrast, the Lions had settled on their best combination before the First Test. The sole change in the pack was an enforced one when Gordon Brown missed the Fourth Test because of injury and was replaced by Chris Ralston. In the backs I took over from Billy Steele on the wing for the last two Tests but as I have said that was partly because the selectors felt it was necessary to have a back-up goal-kicker to Phil Bennett. I had a slightly longer range than Phil but I have not the slightest doubt that my presence did not exactly alter the course of history. I won an award for the most improved player on the tour but such was my form in the first few matches that it would have been well nigh impossible not to have improved!

Despite the fact that victory had eluded us in the Fourth Test we had another rousing party that night. The anticipation of the homeward journey was in the forefront of our minds. Slattery had booked a cabaret which failed to materialize. But as luck would have it Jimmy Logan, the Scottish comedian, was a guest in our hotel and he was prevailed upon to join the party as lead singer. The most poignant moment, however, came when Willie John stood up to sing. No one would admit it but I'd be prepared to bet that there were a few moist eyes in the audience. McBride had been through so many battles with the Lions, many of them losing ones, and there wasn't one person present in that room who now begrudged him his greatest triumph. He seemed to speak for British and Irish rugby when he said, 'Now I can die happy.'

11

To New Zealand in 1977

By 1977 my critical faculties were more highly developed. Furthermore, my sights were set higher. It was no longer enough to be in the Lions party, this time for New Zealand. I was anxious to be in the Test side from the outset and to be a major influence in it. The domestic season had gone well for me, and my chances of going to New Zealand as the first choice full back had been greatly improved by J.P.R. Williams's decision not to tour. Had he made himself available I do not doubt that he would have been the number one full back.

I have always had grave reservations about criticizing selectors. They are easy prey and the side has yet to be picked which has gained unanimous approval. But there were selections made on that tour with which I could not, and still cannot agree. The decision to take David Burcher, the Welsh centre at the expense of Jim Renwick, mystified me. Renwick had been in vintage form that season and quite simply was in a different class. He would have brought pace and a variety to a three-quarter line which was physically well equipped but wholly predictable. In the event, Renwick's presence would probably have made little or no difference to the outcome of the Test series, but his omission was a sad mistake, one of many made before and during that tour.

Tragically, the Lions had been denied the services of Mervyn Davies, the world's finest number 8, and the outstanding candidate for the captaincy. He had captained Wales to the international championship the previous season but at his peak had suffered a brain haemorrhage which ended his rugby career and at one stage threatened his life. In the end the choice lay between Phil Bennett of Wales and the Englishman Roger Uttley. Bennett won the vote whilst Uttley, crippled by a back injury on the eve of departure, was replaced in the party by Jeff Squire. To me Bennett was never the dominant force that McBride had been in South Africa. He missed the presence of senior pros like Gareth Edwards and Ian McLauchlan whose advice and encouragement had meant so much to him in South Africa. It may have been that Phil found the responsibilities of captaincy too much for him, but despite the criticism of him on that tour, many of which were grossly unfair in my opinion, on the field of play, I considered him to be one of the better captains I had played with. We were on the same wavelength. As had happened in South Africa, I made a wretched start to the New Zealand tour but in his own quiet way Benny convinced me that I should relax and play my natural game.

Benny was unfortunate in two respects. The first and most important was the appalling weather which gradually eroded team morale. The second was team selection. He was given a pack of forwards who had power and strength but lacked pace. It wasn't until the belated introduction of Tony Neary to the Test pack that the Lions backs began to function effectively. Fergus Slattery who, along with Davies had been so crucial to the Lions in South Africa, was unavailable, so was Peter Dixon, and Gareth Jenkins, the highly promising Llanelli flanker, had been injured. There was less of a shortage at lock forward but here again I doubted that the selectors had struck the right balance. Geoff Wheel, Nigel Horton, Allan Martin and Gordon Brown were the locks originally selected, with Moss Keane replacing the unfortunate Wheel before the party left for New Zealand. Bill Beaumont, who had played a significant role in a strong England pack that season, was in fact the sixth choice but came out as Horton's replacement and played in three of the four Tests.

The fact that Wales had won the Triple Crown was of course reflected in the selection with 18 Welshmen making the party before the end of the tour. John Dawes, an outstanding captain of the 1971 side, was the obvious choice as coach, and with Dod Burrell, going as manager, and Bennett as captain, the four home unions had stuck by the management formula which had guided the Lions to their first-ever Test series victory over New Zealand in 1971. Unfortunately, Dawes, Burrell and Bennett were not the blend that James, Smith and Dawes had been six years previously. There seemed to be a reluctance on the management's part to be associated in any way with the 1971 Tour. The treatment of Mike Gibson, who to my mind possessed the shrewdest rugby brain in the party, was a case in point. He was shunned by the management and his views seldom if ever sought. Against that there was no doubt that Gibson was past his peak. He had lost some of his pace and was less inclined to involve himself in the physical side of the game. Nevertheless, he still had some valid points to make and could have been an invaluable member of the side.

Few would quibble that our Test front row of Price, Wheeler and Cotton were the best available and very possibly the best ever. They toiled magnificently at the pithead but there were doubts about the supporting cast. Ian McLauchlan, a formidable cornerstone of Lions packs in 1971 and 1974, might justifiably have felt aggrieved by his omission in favour of Clive Williams, especially in view of the fact that the Scottish front row had given the Welsh a roasting at Murrayfield earlier that season. Bobby Windsor, who had gone as first choice hooker, was eventually supplanted by Wheeler and thereafter lost heart. He was a pale shadow of the character who had brightened our duller moments in South Africa.

He, like a number of others in New Zealand, retreated into his shell and succumbed to homesickness. This left Maurice Ignatius Keane unrivalled as the 'tour character'. His attitude was so refreshing. He refused to take anything seriously, and my memory of him is with a smile on his face and a pint of beer in his hand. What he lacked in skill on the field he made up for in spirit. He was one of the most wholehearted players I have ever known and was clearly loved by the players if not always by hotel managers. I recall one particular evening following a good win. Mossy had played well and was in full cry. He had enjoyed an ample sufficiency of food and ale. An excellent evening was drawing to its close when Moss announced his intentions to entertain us with his party trick. His props were four glasses, two of which were filled with water, a tray, two eggs and a brush. A recipe for disaster surely. But no. To everyone's amazement Moss displayed the dexterity of a Paul Daniels and somehow managed to get the eggs into the proper receptacles without a drop of water being spilt or a glass broken. 'And now', said a jubilant Moss, 'for my next trick.' Whereupon he grabbed hold of a tablecloth on top of which were bottles of red wine and port. 'Don't worry,' he said soothingly to those who were sitting round the table, 'stay where you are while I whip away the cloth and leave the bottles standing on the table.' Having seen him perform his first trick so successfully his audience were reassured. Their faith was sadly misguided. Bottles flew in all directions, while Mossy, who had known all along that his party piece was doomed to failure, enjoyed the joke hugely. Throughout the tour there was more than a faint suspicion that Moss was the phantom setter-off of fire alarms. It could never be proved conclusively but in recognition of his services he was presented with a toy fire engine and a fireman's hat on his 29th birthday which, by happy chance, fell midway through the tour.

The standard of food and hotel accommodation were, generally speaking, far below those in South Africa where the quality was five star from first to last. But New Zealand, a comparatively poor country, does not have the same resources. Some of the country towns had advanced very little from the days of the Gold Rush and were not equipped to cope with the needs of a modern touring side. This was interpreted by some of the players as meanness on the part of our hosts. Unfairly so, because the Kiwi generosity of spirit is the equal of any country in the world. They could not be held responsible for a quality of life which is lower than that enjoyed by some of the wealthier countries. Even so these minor annoyances, combined with the incessant rain, contributed to the fact that, socially, the tour was much less enjoyable than its predecessor in South Africa.

My decision to make myself available to tour had not been an automatic one. My wife Audrey was expecting our first child, who was due to be born during the tour. Obviously, I would have liked to have been at home with Audrey and to have been present at the birth. But we discussed the matter fully and agreed that I should go. Because of this I was determined that, from a personal point of view, the tour should be a success. To have made such a sacrifice and not to have done justice to myself would be doubly disappointing. The New Zealand Union was extremely generous. As the birthdate approached they allowed me to phone home almost at will. Peter Wild, our liaison officer, was particularly helpful in this respect and I was very grateful to him for his understanding.

John Dawes has been criticized as being something of a martinet on the training field. But, as I have explained elsewhere in the book, punishing training sessions held no terrors for me. I approached the tour as a job of work, regarding it as my duty both to myself and to my team mates to train as hard and to play as well as I possibly could. It was no hardship, therefore, when I was called upon to play in the first five matches in the tour, twice coming on as a replacement for Bruce Hay. The opening match against Wairarapa-Bush played in the glutinous mud at Masterton had been won with such consummate ease that it hardly prepared us for the next game against Hawkes Bay. The provincial side gave a typically rousing performance, encouraged, no doubt, by the Lions failure to perform some of the basic skills. Gordon

Brown was suffering from a heavy cold and was well below par. Our scrummage superiority was never turned to advantage, our back play was inconsistent. Speaking afterwards George Burrell got the biggest round of applause when he joked 'I would like to pay tribute to the various Walls who took part in today's game – to Murray Wall, to Harry Wall and above all to that bloody great brick wall that Hawkes Bay built across the field!'

We came across a few more brick walls before the First Test, one exception being the fifth match against Wanganui/King Country at Taumaranui. For once it was dry and we recorded our biggest win of the tour by 60 points to 9. I scored five tries which was pretty meaningless against such poor opposition, but it was fun.

Even at this early stage, however, it was beginning to dawn on me that there were some very important differences between this tour and the South African trip. To begin with the New Zealanders, unlike the South Africans, were thoroughly well prepared. The provincial sides which we played against had all done their homework. They knew our strengths and were quick to spot our weaknesses. In addition, our management lacked the stability of Messrs Thomas, Millar and McBride in South Africa.

But I had no complaints. I had played in seven of the first eight games and after a shaky start was beginning to find my best form. I was rested for the ninth match against the New Zealand Universities, which was played at Christchurch on the Tuesday before the First Test. The result shook us to our very roots. A combination of lethargy, complacency perhaps, and some inspired play by the Universities led to the Lions first provincial defeat since South Africa in 1968. This was hardly the best preparation for the Test.

To make matters worse it was not at all certain that the selectors had settled on their Test team. Injuries had hampered them to a certain extent. Neither Gordon Brown nor Nigel Horton was fit, and injury had checked the progress of Derek Quinnell who had been so highly

rated by the All Blacks in 1971. To be perfectly honest I
had no great faith in the pack they selected. Terry
Cobner was enjoying an outstanding tour and was a
marvellous leader but we were critically short of pace in
the back row where Trevor Evans was preferred to Tony
Neary, the one really fast loose forward. Our backs,
individually sound players, were never the force that the
backs had been in South Africa although I could never
agree with the criticisms of Phil Bennett's play. I felt that
he played remarkably well given the additional burden of
captaincy and the atrocious weather conditions.

The All Blacks did not have all their troubles to seek.
Grant Batty was reported to be operating on greatly
reduced power following his tour to South Africa the
previous year when he had damaged knee ligaments.
They also lacked a consistently reliable goal kicker, a
department in which we were unusually strong. In
addition to Benny and myself we had Douglas Morgan
and Steve Fenwick and apart from Morgan the rest of us
were in the side for the Wellington Test. So much rain
fell on Athletic Park during the 36 hours before the game
that the New Zealand Rugby Union hired a helicopter to
dry out the pitch. On the day itself the wind whistled in
from the South and remained for the whole of the match,
but despite its advantage in the first half we turned
round 16–12 down.

In that period the All Blacks scored three tries to nil,
two of which could only be described as flukes. We began
well enough when the All Blacks were penalized at the
first line-out of the match. I kicked the penalty. Then Sid
Going with a typical piece of sorcery found a path
through our pack and scored a try which was, psychologically, the most important of the match. It proved to
the All Blacks that they could score into the wind and
that they could win the game before half-time. Our
scrummaging was infinitely better than the All Blacks
but we were taking a terrible beating in the line-outs
where Moss Keane got no change from Frank Oliver and
the combination of Haden, Kirkpatrick and Lawrie

Knight overwhelmed Allan Martin and Willie Duggan.

But at least we got back in the lead with two penalties by Phil Bennett. Then came the first of the All Blacks lucky breaks. They were awarded a penalty which Bryan Williams felt was within his range. His kick was never in any danger of going over but held up in the wind long enough for the All Blacks forwards to get underneath it. We were so woefully short of defensive cover close to our posts that Brad Johnstone caught the ball and fell over the line. Benny kicked another goal to give us the lead for the third time before the turning point of the match. Brynmor Williams launched our best attacking move to that point. Trevor Evans was put in possession and outside him he had a full three-quarter line with a four to one overlap. We seemed certain to score. Unfortunately the one All Black was Grant Batty who sensed that if he was to save the situation he would have to commit himself totally to an interception. He was helped by the fact that Evans fractionally delayed the delivery of his pass and Batty was off up field with a clear run for the line. Even so, he was 50 yards out and it was a measure of his shortage of pace that Graham Price, chasing back in a hopeless cause, stayed with him every yard of the way. Batty touched down underneath the post, Williams converted and what should have been six points to us, was six points to them. A 12-point try and the difference between victory and defeat.

Now, at least, we knew what to expect from the All Blacks in the weeks ahead. We approached the Second Test at Christchurch in a happier frame of mind. Our Test side was more settled. Bill Beaumont was a revelation; Fran Cotton had returned to top form and had been switched to the loose head; Peter Wheeler had taken Windsor's place as hooker and Derek Quinnell was selected ahead of Trevor Evans. I still did not believe that the selectors had found the right combination in the back row. Quinnell, Cobner and Duggan were basically blind sides or number 8s and none had the pace or creative qualities of Tony Neary.

157

At this stage of the tour our management were expressing reservations about the standards of refereeing in New Zealand. In those days of course the international matches were refereed not by an independent referee but by an official from the host country. I have always taken the view that most referees must be pretty decent sorts. After all it is not everyone who is prepared to sacrifice his free time so that 30 blokes can enjoy themselves. It has been my experience that the vast majority are fair-minded men of integrity who would never wilfully cheat. Perhaps I am not the best judge of such matters. Referees are more often called upon to arbitrate amongst the forwards than they are the backs who might occasionally knock the ball on but who seldom indulge in skulduggery to the same extent as the forwards. In New Zealand, in my humble opinion, I felt the standard of refereeing was very respectable. That said, the Second Test was an extremely physical and occasionally unpleasant affair. I will never forget coming back into the changing room at the end of the game and seeing the exhaustion on the faces of our forwards. They were too tired to acclaim our victory.

The Lions had not been firing on all cylinders up to this point. We were second favourites for the Test but were confident that we could build up on the scrummaging platform we had achieved in Wellington. The All Blacks were clearly worried by our strength in this department and spent much of their time in practice on the scrummaging machine which we were told won the tight head count 5–0! We were also confident that we would put up a better show in the line-outs. Gordon Brown was fit again and Bill Beaumont had shown in a relatively short space of time that he was in awe of no one. He could look after himself. Cotton's presence gave us more bulk at the front of the line and Quinnell would stand no nonsense further back. The withdrawal of Bruce Robertson, the All Black centre, on the eve of the match was another bonus for us. We knew that the series was doomed if we lost this one. Again the pitch had been reduced to a morass of mud by heavy rain which, as it turned out, inconvenienced the All Blacks in the scrummage more than it did the Lions.

New Zealand were given an early opportunity to take the lead when Bryan Williams, never more than an auxiliary place-kicker, made a hash of an easy penalty kick. Psychologically this miss was almost as much of a boost to us as Sid Going's try had been to New Zealand at Athletic Park. We began to win the line-outs and Benny kicked sensibly and shrewdly, exposing the limitations of Colin Farrell at full back. It was Benny who kicked us ahead with a penalty in the first ten minutes and not long afterwards J.J. Williams dummied, stepped inside the All Blacks cover and scored a great try. Benny increased our lead with his second and third penalties and remarkably we were 13–3 ahead. The All Blacks began to lose their self-control. There was much indiscriminate punching in which Kevin Eveleigh, the All Black flank forward, played a prominent and demeaning part. Bryan Williams was successful with a couple of penalties before half-time and one after the interval but missed several other attempts in the second half, one of which very nearly hit the corner flag. Their team work began to disintegrate. Sid Going, great player that he was, took rather too much on himself and, to our intense surprise and relief, played himself out of the side for the Third Test.

We had learned our lessons from our first encounter with Sid, and had determined that he was not going to receive anything like the same freedom at Christchurch that he enjoyed in Wellington. The All Blacks, as you would expect, fought on to the bitter end but our defence absorbed the pressure and when the final whistle went we knew that we had saved the tour from a long, lingering death. The Maoris, Waikato, New Zealand Juniors and Auckland were the hurdles between the Second and Third Tests when we began to display our best form. Indeed I would go so far as to say that the 1977 Lions showed much more imagination and enterprise behind the scrum than the 1974 vintage, especially on the few occasions when we were blessed with firm pitches.

The victory over a powerful Auckland side by 34 points to 15 was possibly our finest display. The sun was shining, there was a light breeze and Eden Park has seldom looked more inviting. I remember too that it was Tony Neary's first Saturday match. He was also appointed pack leader, and how well he responded to the challenge. He was easily the most constructive forward we had in the party and it was Neary I had to thank for one of my two tries that day. Our forwards annihilated the Auckland pack, a number of whom had been making some rather rash predictions before the match. Eric Boggs, the Auckland coach, actually went as far as to say that the Lions were the worst touring side he had seen. I think he had changed his mind long before the final whistle.

We felt that we deserved our short break in the beautiful Bay of Islands despite the ever-present threat of rain. For three days before the crucial Third Test in Dunedin we had the opportunity to refresh our minds and bodies and to contemplate the astonishing news that the New Zealand selectors had dropped Sid Going. I thought he was the single most important member of the All Blacks side. Doug Bruce was a stand off of average ability, and Colin Farrell a fairly ordinary full back. Bryan Williams had lost a yard of pace which meant that the All Blacks' back play revolved around the solid centre partnership of Bill Osborne and Bruce Robertson and the guile of Sid Going. He had been tormenting British teams for a decade and now at last we were rid of him. His replacement was the Canterbury half-back Lyn Davis, an immensely experienced and thoroughly competent player but hardly in Going's class as a strategist.

Our injury list was lengthening alarmingly. Brynmor Williams, Derek Quinnell and Terry Cobner had all been laid up and Clive Williams, whose ligaments had been torn, would take no further part in the tour. The only cheerful news around this time was that Charlie Faulkner, the third member of the Pontypool front row, was on his way out as a replacement – news which, at last, brought a smile to Bobby Windsor's face.

The All Blacks could not have made a more encouraging start. Ford, the new cap on the left wing, set up a maul, the backs handled and Bruce Robertson kicked over my head. Kirkpatrick, a superb forward in any era, won the race to the touchdown. Bevan Wilson, one of five new caps in this side, converted with his first kick in international rugby. Unfortunately, it was not to be our day for goal-kicking. Both Benny and I missed very kickable penalties at crucial times during the match – six out of seven attempts – which must have been discouraging for our forwards who once again severely embarrassed the All Blacks in the set piece. We had so many chances to win, and to this day I am not entirely sure how we managed to lose 19–7. Willie Duggan scored our try and I did eventually kick a penalty but with so much possession we should have won handsomely. One thing in our favour though – we gave Bevan Wilson one of the easiest baptisms in the history of international rugby! Our tactical kicking was inept and our insistence on holding the ball in the back row of the scrum did nothing to ease the pressure on our half-backs. As it was, Brynmor Williams was suffering from a recurrence of his hamstring injury, and J.J. Williams hobbled off to be replaced by Ian McGeechan.

We were 10–7 down when Benny missed a penalty from point blank range. Our forwards looked on in disbelief. They were giving the All Black pack a pasting. I remember Gordon Brown who was playing Andy Haden off the park, shouting to us 'Come on boys, we've got them. Look at them – they're knackered!' Five minutes later the game and victory in the series were beyond our reach. Wilson kicked a penalty from 45 yards. Then Graham Mourie, who had hitherto been channelling all his very considerable skills into defence, burst out in support of a couple of rare New Zealand attacks. From one, Wilson landed another mighty penalty and from the other Robertson dropped a goal. The result bore no relation whatsoever to the pattern of play and was cruel reward for our forwards. But by now it was obvious that one of the basic theories of international rugby – win the forward battle and win the game – had been exploded once and for all.

Our sole aim now was to save the series. We began with a comfortable win over Counties – Thames Valley at Pukekohe with the Scots very much to the fore. Dougie Morgan scored 19 points and Bruce Hay got a couple of tries. North Auckland were next on the list although our victory in this game was marred by injuries to Terry Cobner and Derek Quinnell which meant that neither would play again on tour. We lost a couple more men – Mike Gibson and Bruce Hay – in winning the penultimate match against Bay of Plenty. Then it was on to Auckland in preparation for the Fourth, and final, Test. With Cobner and Quinnell *hors de combat*, Tony Neary and Jeff Squire were picked on the flanks, and to my way of thinking the pack was the strongest we had fielded.

The All Blacks seemed to think so too. They had dropped both their props from the Third Test, Bill Bush and John McEldowney, and had restored Kent Lambert and Brad Johnstone. They had also gone to great lengths to keep their training sessions secret. It made no difference. Their forwards were so humiliated that they were reduced at one stage to a three man scrummage. We should have won, of course. But again we missed our chances and ultimately fell to a fortuitous try by Laurie Knight in the closing minutes which denied us a share of the spoils.

My heart bled for Benny after the game. He was shattered both physically and mentally, yet he had to stand up in front of a jubilant crowd at Eden Park and give a speech. Many people criticized him for his performance on that tour both as a player and as a captain. They felt that the pressure of captaincy had had an adverse effect on his play and that he had suffered from scrum halves who were unable to give him either the speed or length of pass he had received from Gareth Edwards with Wales or from his club partner at Llanelli, Selwyn Williams. Admittedly, Benny had given an inexplicably poor performance in the Third Test and had seemed overwhelmed by the cares of the world and captaincy and perhaps a touch of homesickness in the closing stages, but I considered that, as a player, he was one of the real successes. Every time he got the ball he threatened danger particularly on the firmer grounds. Our wounds may, to some extent, have been self-inflicted but we did not deserve to lose that series, and in making a proper assessment of the tour it has to be said that the All Blacks were no bad side. I would go as far as to say that they were stronger than the 1971 All Blacks. Bryan Williams was still a top class wing, Robertson and Osborne were the finest pair of centres fielded by New Zealand for 20 years, and Sid Going, as I have said, was a match winner. It would have been hard to find a better back-row combination than Mourie, Knight and Kirkpatrick. Oliver and Haden were surely as fine a pair of locks as have ever played for New Zealand. It was only in the front row that the All Blacks were vulnerable.

The Lions failed because they could not turn possession into points. The back play has been criticized, justifiably so I suppose, although I felt that our backs were every bit as skilled as the All Blacks. I struck up a good rapport with my wings and in particular with Peter Squires and J.J. Williams. I can only repeat that Benny was a dream to play with. Perhaps we suffered for not having the right blend in the centre, and I certainly believe that it would have made sound rugby logic to have developed attacking strategies from our loose forwards. But that would have required the injection of pace which could only have been provided by Tony Neary. Had Fergus Slattery been available and had he and Neary played on the flanks with either Duggan or Quinnell at number 8 we would probably have won the series.

163

Judged by the ultimate yardstick of the Test series the tour was a failure, but for my own part I enjoyed it. Unlike the 1974 tour I was totally involved. I played in 14 matches including all four Tests, and was given freedom to run. I was lucky enough to be the top try scorer with 11 tries, and felt that I was making an important contribution. I cannot subscribe to the criticisms of John Dawes. You must judge a person as you find him, and I have no axe to grind. He gave me a free rein. At no time did he dictate how I should play the game and was big enough to admit that I knew more about full back play than he would ever know. I respected him for that.

12

South Africa Again

To my surprise and disappointment, when the Lions party to tour South Africa was announced, I was selected not as a full back but as one of the three wings along with Mike Slemen and John Carleton. I felt that after eight years of international rugby I had done enough to establish myself as the resident full back in the UK. The selection was all the more unfathomable in view of the fact that we were going to South Africa where the conditions suited an attacking full back. But for all their many other qualities neither Bruce Hay nor Rodney O'Donnell, the two full backs chosen, was best known for his attacking qualities.

The party was chosen the day after England had won the Grand Slam by beating Scotland at Murrayfield. It was clear, therefore, that England's success would be reflected in the composition of the party and sure enough, even without Tony Neary and Roger Uttley who were unavailable, there were eight Englishmen in the original selection. A horrendous run of injuries saw to it that there were two more before the end of the tour. All four props and both hookers were very well established players, and of the tight five forwards three – Wheeler, Cotton and Beaumont – were world-class. Sadly, we were not so well blessed with back-row forwards. It was impossible to conceal the absence of speed merchants like Tony Neary and David Leslie especially on the fast going surfaces in South Africa.

The fact was that we had no one to match the South Africa flanker Rob Louw who dominated this series in much the way that Jock Hobbs was to upstage the 1983 Lions in New Zealand, and the way in which Fergus Slattery controlled the 1974 tour. Our problems in this area were exacerbated by the injury at the beginning of the tour to Stuart Lane, a flanker of real pace. David Leslie was the man they wanted to replace Lane but he had been troubled by injury for most of that season and felt unable to make the trip. But at that time in his career he was faster and hungrier than he was when he played such a significant role in Scotland's Grand Slam season in 1984. Had I been a selector I think I would have done everything in my power to persuade Slattery and Neary to change their minds. With either one of them the course of the series might well have been altered.

As it was, we went into the Tests with a back row combination permed from Jeff Squire, Derek Quinnell, John O'Driscoll and Colm Tucker – all admirable players in their own ways but none of them having the pace so necessary to set up good loose possession. Quinnell, a magnificent forward in his prime, was no longer in that state of grace, and in my opinion should not have been selected. It was also something of a mystery to some of us why Gordon Brown had not been selected. Admittedly he had played little competitive rugby that season but Brown had proved on three previous occasions that he was in his element on major tours. There was no doubt that he had played his best rugby for the Lions and, unlike some of those selected, he had been to the summit before and knew what to expect.

There could, however, be no misgivings about the two scrum halves who were the best I have toured with. Both Terry Holmes and Colin Patterson were players of the highest class, and if Holmes had the edge it could not have been by very much. Patterson was devastatingly agile and, for a man of such small stature, remarkably strong. Both fly halves, Ollie Campbell and Gareth Davies, were automatic certainties although here again I felt that the selectors might have taken the bold course and gambled on John Rutherford. Rutherford had only recently been introduced to international rugby but I really believed that he had already shown enough form and potential to be selected at fly-half ahead of both Campbell and Davies. At very worst he was light years in front of Peter Morgan who was selected as the utility back. There was no limit to what he might have achieved on the unyielding South African grounds and in any case there was more than a faint suspicion of doubt that Davies was not fully fit. Three weeks before the Lions party was selected he had limped off the field with a hamstring injury and had announced to the waiting press that this would be his last game before the Lions tour. Did he have some prior knowledge of the team, or was he just immensely confident that he would be selected?

The wings John Carleton and Mike Slemen were out of the top drawer, and had I been a selector I would have picked them ahead of me in the Test side. I did not rate myself highly as a winger and never enjoyed playing in the position. In 1974 I had been quite content to tour South Africa in J. P. R.'s shadow, but in 1980 I felt very strongly that I should have been selected as a full back. At no time, however, did I consider making myself unavailable for the tour and I was fairly confident that once I got out there I would prove the selectors wrong. My aim was to make myself indispensable to the side in the role of an attacking full back. But the best-laid plans...

A week after the Lions party was announced I departed with the Scottish Co-optimists for the Hong Kong Sevens, an event which was to capture the imagination of the rugby world, and one which I had looked forward to immensely and was not about to abandon even for a forthcoming Lions tour. In the semi-final against New Zealand I tore a hamstring, but as there was a six-week gap before the Lions left I was not unduly concerned. The injury responded well to treatment – so well that I was encouraged to step up my training schedule. In my eagerness to outstrip nature I

167

overstretched at a sprint and felt an ominous twinge of pain from the hamstring. That meant another two-week rest and by now time was a problem. I was concerned that I was going on a major tour well short of the necessary fitness. Two days before departure I went running again. Again I felt the tugging discomfort of the hamstring. Even so, I was hopeful that they would take me. I knew that I would be unable to play for the first couple of weeks but that with the right treatment and a gradual build-up to fitness I would be 100 per cent fit after three weeks. I wouldn't have been the first mildly crocked player to set off from Heathrow on a Lions tour.

Our management team was Syd Millar the manager, Noel Murphy the coach and, for the first time on a Lions tour, an official doctor – Jack Matthews, the famous Welsh centre of the 1950s. As events turned out he was to be the most overworked member of the party. He gave me a detailed examination after which he reported back to Millar that in his opinion it would be two to three weeks before I'd be fit to play. Millar, therefore, decided that it would be putting undue pressure on the players who would have to cover for me during that period and that they should call up a replacement. No one could quibble with Millar's decision – he was merely working within the guidelines laid down – but I felt that he might have risked taking me. Then again, it all depends on how highly the management rated my importance to the side. My replacement was the Welsh wing, Elgan Rees.

Millar's appointment as manager was, like Davies's apparently had been at stand off, a foregone conclusion. It would certainly have been hard to find someone better qualified to do the job. He had won 37 Irish caps, had been on three Lions tours as a player, and most important of all had coached the 1974 Lions in South Africa. Moreover, although as a player he had made his reputation as a prop forward, in the early part of his rugby career he had played at scrum half, stand off and centre, and therefore had more than a passing acquaintance with back play. Murphy had enjoyed a similarly distinguished playing career as a wing forward, winning 41 Irish caps and twice touring with the Lions. He had enjoyed some success as a coach with the Irish side and was generally highly respected.

It fell to Millar to break the news to me that I would not be going. As I say, I could not blame him for making the decision but the irony of the situation was that Ollie Campbell pulled a hamstring in the first week of training and when I did eventually join the party as a replacement he had played in only one game. The decision was made at a London hotel on the day of departure and for me there was the slightly embarrassing position of having waved goodbye to family, friends and photographers at Edinburgh Airport in the morning and then returning home that evening. I was desperately disappointed, frustrated and a little annoyed. The management, I felt, could have taken a more lenient approach.

There was nothing for it but to accept the judgement, so I returned home to rest the injury for three weeks, monitoring the tour by reading the newspapers and listening to the radio commentaries of the Saturday matches. The Lions were pursued by wretched luck. In the first minute of the first match against Eastern Province, Stuart Lane, dashing off the back of a line-out, stumbled as he made to tackle Gavin Cowley, the Eastern Province fly half, and tore the lateral ligaments in his right knee. His tour was over and the Lions were left without a specialist open-side flanker. Lane was soon joined in the dressing room by Gareth Davies who dislocated a shoulder. Victory, by 28 points to 16, was therefore achieved at considerable cost. Despite the injuries it was clear that the Lions had several major problems to sort out before the tour gathered pace. Terry Holmes had been given a fearful battering by the opposition forwards streaming through the line-out. The scrummage, rock solid from first to last in 1974, had by all accounts lacked control and had been too easily disrupted by a mediocre provincial pack. I read in some newspaper reports that Bruce Hay had been in extreme difficulty at full back due, in a very large part, to the conditions. It takes time to become accustomed to the glare of the South African sun which can distort distances and cause misjudgements under the high ball.

Furthermore, the Lions had to contend with Dennis Campher, a wildly indisciplined centre, in the ranks of the opposition. He fully deserved the nickname that the Lions gave him of 'Dennis the Menace'. He all but decapitated Slemen, late-tackled Rees and provided the finishing touches to Gareth Davies's discomfort. It struck me even at that stage in the tour that with a few more Camphers, some weak refereeing and some hard grounds, there would be a steady flow of replacements leaving from the UK.

The next game, against an invitation XV, brought more woe to the Lions. Phil Blakeway, the Lions tight head, left the field before the end clutching the ribs which had been causing him pain all season and which had required pain killing injections before two of England's internationals. For Blakeway, as it had been for Lane in the previous game, the tour was over. Before the First Test they would be joined by Terry Holmes who in his five games scored three tries and began to stir memories of Gareth Edwards in 1974. A replacement was also going to be required at stand off now that neither Davies nor Campbell, who had not shaken off the effects of his hamstring injury, was likely to be fit for the First Test.

Had the Lions been looking for a purely attacking player then they must have gone for John Rutherford but in Campbell's absence the priority was for a goal-kicker. Tony Ward was the obvious choice, although there were dark tales amongst the Irish contingent that Murphy would not countenance Ward's presence in the Irish side because he considered him too selfish. Be that as it may the circumstances were desperate enough for Murphy to subordinate any personal feelings he may have harboured towards Ward. Ward was sent for and so was Ian Stephens, the Bridgend prop, as Blakeway's replacement.

The Lions' troubles continued. Fran Cotton left the field at Stellenbosch with respiratory problems and the Lions' choice for the First Test was very different from the one envisaged by the selectors at the start of the tour. O'Donnell was at full back. Ward and Patterson were the half-backs; Clive Williams was on the loose head and O'Driscoll, Squire and Quinnell were a powerful if somewhat ponderous and unbalanced back-row combination.

The First Test was played at Newlands, Cape Town, in superb conditions. In Edinburgh that Saturday I had taken myself down to Meggetland, home of the Boroughmuir Club who were hosting a summer challenge – a fun event where the Edinburgh rugby clubs competed against each other at various sports. I had begun training again more with a view to keeping myself in trim than with any thought of going out to South Africa as a replacement. I was lying on the grass watching the tennis and listening to the radio commentary from Cape Town.

The Springboks were slight favourites in the pre-match assessments principally because the Lions had not been thoroughly convincing in their early matches and because the Springboks were fielding Naas Botha, whose goal-kicking exploits had astonished the rugby world. In 53 first-class games he had scored 661 points, averaging 12.5 points a game. In five games that season he had scored 72 points. Against him the Lions put up Ward who, almost a year ago to the day in Australia, had been ousted from the Irish side by Campbell. Ward was both hero and villain in Cape Town. His 18 points from five penalty goals and a drop goal broke the points scoring record for a Lion held by Tom Kiernan, but unfortunately Ward played no small part in two of the Springboks' five tries.

The scoring pattern and the closeness of the contest, intriguing as it was, did not capture my attention so much as the news that John Carleton had suffered a rib injury and been taken off the field. Suddenly it dawned on me that I might be called out to replace him. Sure

171

enough, I had not been back in the house for half an hour when the phone rang. 'Can you come out to join us immediately?' asked the beleaguered Millar anxiously. 'Sure,' I replied, 'I heard about Carleton's injury.' 'It's not Carleton you'll be replacing,' said Millar. 'It's Mike Slemen. His wife is not well and he's going back home to be with her.' I left London on the Tuesday and joined the Lions in Johannesburg the following day. To my astonishment I was told that I would be playing that Saturday against Transvaal – at full back. I could hardly believe my luck. I knew that neither Bruce Hay nor Rodney O'Donnell had been playing particularly well at full back, but the match against Transvaal was one of the most important provincial ones of the tour so it seemed logical that the selectors were seriously considering me as the Test full back. Naturally I was delighted. My pleasure at the news and my subsequent enjoyment of the game itself, in which we played quite brilliantly for the first half, was soured by the fact that I tweaked my hamstring – not the one which had caused all the bother before the tour but the one in my left leg. We also lost David Richards for the rest of the tour which meant another replacement.

I did not know it then, but I was to be hampered by hamstring injuries throughout the tour. I could never get properly fit which was both annoying and frustrating. For the first 30 minutes of the game against Transvaal I was running everything – right, left and centre. It was exhilarating stuff. But then my hamstring went and I was seldom able to operate at full strength. Throughout the tour a pattern emerged. I played in a game but couldn't train during the week because of the tightness in my legs. I did no sprinting but received physiotherapy three or four times a week and ended up getting a cortisone injection before the final Test. By the end I could fairly be described as a limping disaster with both hamstrings and two Achilles tendons playing up.

My own assessment of the First Test, admittedly from the safe distance of 6,000 miles, had been that the

Springboks, who scored five tries to one, were well worthy of their victory and that the five-point margin between the sides had flattered the Lions. But on the evidence of our game against Transvaal who had been rated as one of the top provincial sides in the country, I felt that the Test series could still be won. Given that the horrific run of injuries had come to a halt, the selectors could perhaps settle on a regular Test combination which presumably would not be too far removed from the one which had routed Transvaal 32–12.

Originally the Lions itinerary included a match against Zimbabwe in Salisbury but on the advice of the Zimbabwean Government the local union had reluctantly decided to call it off. It was a great sadness for those players who had not previously experienced a visit to that magnificent country.

The replacement fixture against Eastern Transvaal at Springs was hardly an attractive alternative. Springs is an industrial town, forbidding and depressing, some 30 miles from Johannesburg. By way of compensation however the Lions played the Springboks at cricket. Our victory by five wickets may have had something to do with a sparkling 79 scored by a guest player named Graeme Pollock. Peter Wheeler, keeping wicket in a pair of flannels at least three sizes too small, gave a brilliant impression of the proverbial cat on a hot tin roof, John Robbie, the replacement scrum half for Holmes, caused the management's hearts to miss a beat when he tripped over a water hydrant, and Chris Lander of the *Daily Mirror* returned career best bowling figures of 2 for 32 off one over.

From what I could gather from reports and from the evidence of television, the Lions had fallen on their own sword in the First Test. They had made far too many basic errors and had made the Springboks look much better than they really were. Gysie Pienaar played like Superman at full back largely because of Ward's indiscreet kicking out of hand and Gerrie Germishuys, a seasoned compaigner but a wing of only moderate ability, looked a world beater.

173

From a personal point of view I felt reasonably confident of winning a Test place at full back. Bruce Hay was playing well on the wing and seemed certain to be selected for the Second Test in that position, Rodney O'Donnell, on the other hand, had not enjoyed his first taste of rugby at Test level. At Newlands he had fielded well and had displayed all the courage in the world. But he was hesitant with the ball in his hands and wayward in his kicking. My chief concern, however, was with my own fitness. Since the First Test the Lions had bade farewell to three more players – Slemen, Richards and Holmes – but had been encouraged by the fact that John Carleton had fought through the pain barrier of a serious rib injury to take his place on the right wing. It was a triumph of mind over matter.

As expected Hay took over from Slemen on the left wing. There was a new centre pairing of Clive Wood-ward and Ray Gravell, and Gareth Davies was brought in at stand off to partner the admirable Patterson. The pack was shaping up as a formidable unit although still lacking pace, and was unchanged from the First Test. The Springboks made only one change with Kevin de Klerk, who had played well in the line-out in the Transvaal game, replacing Moaner van Heerden in the second row.

Analysis of the First Test had convinced us that the Springboks had run the ball because we gave them gilt-edged opportunities to do so. We knew that we must not be so profligate again. On the morning of the Second Test which was to be played at Bloemfontein, an article appeared in a local newspaper in which Butch Lochner, the convener of the Springbok selectors, was quoted as saying that the Lions were cheating in the line-outs. There was also a veiled threat that those who lived by the sword could expect to die by the sword. We were unconcerned. Bill Beaumont and Maurice Colclough had been successfully mopping up all resistance in the line-outs, and both could look after themselves. So for that matter could our auxiliary line-out men Squire, Quinnell and O'Driscoll.

As events turned out our forwards held their own but lacked the animal aggression of the Springboks, especially in the loose where Louw and their sturdy blind side Theuns Stofberg were much quicker to the loose ball. In many ways the pattern of play in the Second Test was a carbon copy of the First. Obviously we had not learned from our mistakes. We missed out tackles, kicked indifferently and allowed an uncertain Botha to rediscover his scoring touch. Gradually his 60-yard diagonal kicks sapped the energy from our forwards and the Springboks scored four tries to add to the five they had got at Newlands.

I must take my share of responsibility for the first try which came from a badly directed kick out of defence. The Springboks ran back at us and Willie du Plessis scored in the corner. John O'Driscoll, the outstanding Lions forward on the day, scored a try for us which Davies converted. The next 12 points went to South Africa and proved decisive with Botha kicking two penalties and converting Stoffberg's controversial try. Bruce Hay, whose tackling was immense, brought Ray Mordt down short of the line and Mordt played the ball after it had touched the ground. Francis Palmade, the French referee, waved play on and Stoffberg scored.

Before half-time our injury jinx struck again, Gareth Davies being replaced by Ollie Campbell at stand off. By this time we had come right back into the match and were trailing by just one point at 15–16. In the second half Campbell missed a relatively simple penalty, and two tries within a minute, the first by Germishuys and again by Pienaar, sealed our fate. After the game Bill Beaumont was criticized for entrusting the penalty kick to Campbell, who had just come onto the field as a replacement instead of giving it to me. But the truth is that I was far from confident in my own fitness. I was desperately disappointed in my own performance at Bloemfontein. I had grave doubts about my ability to run from deep defensive positions. It wouldn't have been so bad had I been able to train during the week before a game but with the discomfort from my hamstrings and Achilles tendons this was just not possible.

The day before the Bloemfontein Test had been Friday 13 June – a dreadful day for Rodney O'Donnell whose superstitions were becoming a minor sensation in South Africa. He had so many superstitions that he could not always remember them all. He would refuse to walk on lines and could be seen in hotel foyers zig-zagging across the lined carpets; he had to be last onto the bus, last into the changing room and last onto the field. He would not go onto the field three times, a foible which had caused all manner of problems earlier that season when Ireland had played France. Having walked onto the field for the customary pre-match inspection he was then called out for the team photograph. This he steadfastly refused to do until Noel Murphy undertook full responsibility for whatever misfortune befell him during the game. This apparently pacified O'Donnell, and he lined up with the rest of the team for the photograph. There were innumerable other weird superstitions all of which had to be observed at one time or another during his day.

It was only natural, therefore, that Friday the 13th was a day which we could not allow to pass unnoticed and unmarked. By seven in the morning ladders had been erected outside Rodney's bedroom door, lines marked on the carpets and pieces of paper with the number 13 fixed to all lift buttons. Needless to say it was a bad time for poor Rodney. By evening he had lost his watch and wallet and by the middle of the following week he was lying in hospital with a dislocated neck. He was the eighth player to have been struck down by some misfortune since the party had left London in May, but serious though his injury was, O'Donnell could count himself very lucky that he was alive.

We were playing the Junior Springboks. I was on the left wing, with O'Donnell at full back. The opposition looked uncommonly useful for a midweek side. They were captained by Wynand Claasen, a number 8 who was to captain the Springboks later in his career.

Hempes du Toit, another Springbok in the making, who had given Fran Cotton a hard time of it at Stellenbosch, was at tight-head prop, and the back line, which included a young man of raw promise called Danie Gerber, was one of the most exciting we had come up against. It was an excellent match, to my mind the best game of the tour. I had very little to do on the wing in the first half but when I moved to full back to replace O'Donnell things began to happen. O'Donnell's injury was the result of a head-on collision with the powerful Gerber who, need it be said, was wearing the number 13 jersey.

Paul Dodge, who had come out as the replacement centre for David Richards, made his first appearance of the tour that day and played well enough to merit inclusion in the side for the Saturday game against Northern Transvaal which was being billed as the Fifth Test. On our way to Pretoria we had heard the rumour that Fergus Slattery had been asked to come out as O'Donnell's replacement. It seemed a most sensible course of action to take. Our lack of pace at loose forward was proving to be a major handicap both in attack and defence, and both Slattery and Neary had intimated that they would be available in the latter stages of the tour. Whether or not it was ethical to replace a full back with a back-row forward was not a matter which concerned us. In the event the question never arose because Slattery declined the invitation.

Four members of the Northern Transvaal pack had played against us in the Second Test and two others – Geldenhuys and Oberholtzen – had played for the Junior Springboks. The Provincial side was captained by Naas Botha who would be playing in front of his own crowd and with his regular scrum half Tommy du Plessis. Now, we were constantly being told, we would see the real Botha.

The facilities at Loftus Versfeld are superb, surpassed only by the magnificent new stadium at Ellis Park. The ground holds 68,000, all seated, and for this match there was not a seat to be had. It was, therefore, a world record attendance for a provincial match.

In the first half we gave what was very probably our best performance of the tour, scoring 16 points and dominating the forward exchanges. In this period the 'Blue Bulls', as they were nicknamed, were like calves led to the slaughter. Unfortunately, the referee Frik Burger seemed disinclined to award us penalties anywhere else but in our own half. It was from one of the few penalties given to us that I kicked what was undoubtedly the longest goal of my career. We were playing at altitude, of course, but even so the penalty was given well inside our own half – some 60 metres from the post – and the ball was still climbing as it crossed the bar.

We had earned our three-day break in Durban, the highlight of which was the landing of a 26 lb barracuda by Ollie Campbell, a reluctant fisherman and a poor sailor, who had spent most of the trip trying not to be sick. It was a blessed relief to relax on the beach, to swim, to play tennis or golf and to escape from the constant and searching glare of the Press. We were also greatly cheered to hear the news from the Rand Clinic in Johannesburg that Rodney O'Donnell had undergone surgery on his neck injury. The operation, which had involved the grafting of a bone from his hip, had been successful, and although he had now to face the fact that one door in his life had been closed, he realized that he had been an extremely lucky young man.

We could no longer win the series. The best we could do was to share it, and although I still felt that we had the players to win the two remaining Tests I was becoming increasingly aware that we did not have the organization to do so, particularly in the backs. No obvious leader was emerging to take charge of the back play, and it tended to be left to the stand off of the day to run the show. Ray Gravell assumed a kind of responsibility but, delightful man though he is, Gravell does not possess the sharpest analytical mind. In 1974 the back play had been controlled by Edwards and Bennett. In

1977 Bennett and Dawes had been the dominant forces, but in 1980 no leader emerged. Manager, coach and captain were all forwards, and Noel Murphy concentrated nearly all his efforts on forward play.

I was far and away the most senior back and the sole survivor of the 1974 campaign, but with my legs and ankles in such a mess I had too many problems of my own to be an effective organizer of others. Apart from which I was not at all certain what role I was supposed to be playing. I was constantly being switched from full back to wing and back again to full back. Jim Renwick would have been admirably suited to do the job but he was completely out of favour, having lost his place after the First Test at Newlands, and he was only likely to regain it in the event of a plague striking down two-thirds of the team. Certainly I did not feel authoritative enough to run the show. The problem of our ad-hoc arrangement was that in the two Tests we had played three stand offs – Ward, Davies and Campbell – a turnover which hardly made for tactical consistency.

This lack of co-ordination was apparent throughout the tour, not only in our play but also in our training. I was completely mystified by Murphy's failure to insist on sprint training. To me speed is a basic essential whether you are a finely tuned athlete on the wing or a lumbering donkey in the second row. It is always possible to increase one's pace and to sharpen one's reflexes. In 1974 Syd Millar had devoted a part of each session to sprint training with the result that we felt more confident in our running. I am speaking not only for myself when I say that in 1980 the essential ingredient of confidence was in desperately short supply.

Confidence might have made the difference between winning and losing the Third Test at Port Elizabeth. I almost had the destiny of the series in my hands but, trailing 12–10 with minutes left, I could not hold onto a pass which would have put me clear with the Springboks' line at my mercy. The conditions on the day were quite appalling which should have been to our advan-

179

tage. We knew that we would have to apply continuous pressure to the Springboks' defence, something which we had singularly failed to do in the previous matches. We judged that our task would be all the easier with a wet ball and a heavy ground. Our slower, stronger forwards would at last be able to compete with Rob Louw and company.

The selectors had chosen the side originally picked for the Northern Transvaal game the previous week which meant that Colin Patterson was reinstated at scrum half. John Robbie had played at Pretoria because Patterson had been unfit and had given an excellent account of himself. But there was no reason to drop Patterson. He had demonstrated his ability to correct his mistakes and improve his technique. It was hard to believe that Terry Holmes, had he escaped injury, would have been any more effective than this great-hearted Irishman. There were five changes from the side which had lost the Second Test, two of them positional. Paul Dodge came into the centre, and Woodward, his Leicester club-mate, switched to the right wing in place of the unfortunate John Carleton. Ollie Campbell was at stand off and in the back row Colm Tucker was picked on the flank with Jeff Squire moving to number 8 in place of Derek Quinnell.

Morne du Plessis, the Springbok captain, won the toss and chose to play into the wind which, as captain, was always a gamble in as much as you were pilloried if events turned against you. But it is a decision which I have made as captain and would defend on the ground that players very often prefer to face the elements when they are fresh. The onus is then on the opposition to get points on the board before half-time.

We scored our first points in the opening minute when Ollie Campbell kicked a penalty. Unfortunately I missed a couple of penalties in the first half, admittedly from a long way out, but comfortably within my range. But the turning point came much later in the game. We were leading 10–6 going into the final quarter. Botha, who was playing with more composure than he had done in the first two Tests, kicked diagonally over Clive Woodward's head. The ball stopped short of touch and Woodward, with Germishuys breathing down his neck, shepherded the ball over the line. Had he been an experienced wing he would have made sure that he booted it into the back row of the stand to deny the Springboks a quick throw. Worse still, however, Woodward turned his back on Germishuys, who grabbed the ball and threw it to Stoffberg. The flanker made ground before sending a return pass to Germishuys who scored his third try in three Tests. Botha's kick from the touch-line with a heavy ball was perfectly struck.

Once again the Lions had beaten the opposition forwards all ends up but had lost the series. It may be an over simplification but I will go to my grave believing that had the Lions gone for greater mobility in their back row then the 1977 series in New Zealand and the 1980 series in South Africa – especially the latter – would have been won. Nevertheless it is true that at Port Elizabeth we again kicked badly from the hand. Gysie Pienaar, the Springbok full back, was quite rightly later acclaimed as the man of the series, but here again I am convinced that he was vulnerable under pressure and that we made him look a great deal better than he was.

In one respect then the tour was over. We could no longer win the series and the temptation is very strong in such circumstances to lose concentration and to free-wheel, but we believed that we were much too good a side to go home without at least one victory over the Springboks. In the wake of the disappointment at Port Elizabeth we enjoyed our game against the South African Barbarians, a side which had included the great Argentinian stand-off Hugo Porta. I derived particular enjoyment from it because it was a warm sunny day, the Durban ground suited me and we threw the ball around.

Our next game against Western Province was going even better for us. I had scored one of our four tries, dropped a goal and had had a few decent runs but ten

181

minutes from the end that infernal hamstring, which had been threatening trouble for weeks, finally went. To make matters worse my Achilles tendon had come out in sympathy, and I knew that the only cure was a long rest. I discussed the problem with Syd Millar and it was agreed that, instead of going to Kimberley for the next match against Griqualand West, I should return to Johannesburg for treatment. The hope was that with five or six days of intensive treatment on the offending limb I would be fit enough to play in the Fourth Test. I was far from fit as it happened but enthusiasm and cortizone got me out onto the park.

Few people outside our immediate circle gave us much chance of winning the final Test at Loftus Versfeld. No other Lions team in history had done it in South Africa, not even the unbeaten side of 1974. But we did, and what's more we did it despite showing once again our infinite capacity for self-destruction. I did not think we played as well in the Fourth Test as we had done in the two previous games, but strangely it was the Springboks, not the Lions, who appeared jaded and travel-weary.

I scored one try but later in the game I missed a clear chance to score again. I was given the ball 20 yards out and made for the line with Pienaar corner flagging. Had I been half fit I would have made it, but over that distance I was probably half a yard slower than normal which is the difference between success and failure at this level. For me pace maketh confidence, and confidence maketh the player. Will-power and injections can take you so far but in my case it was rather akin to Samson with a toupée. You cannot cheat nature.

It was now undeniably the case that since the early 1970s the quality of British forward play had improved immeasurably. British back play had, however, deteriorated to much the same extent. In South Africa in 1980 the Lions were indisputably the better side but their talents were applied to mediocre effect. It is easy in such circumstances to blame the coach. I would acknowledge that on this tour Noel Murphy concentrated overmuch on the forwards, but I've always held by the view that it is the players and not the coach who win matches. I don't honestly believe that a coach makes the difference between success and failure.

I participated in three Lions tours, two of them losing ones, and the only individual who emerged relatively unscathed from 1977 and 1980 was Bill Beaumont. As a losing captain in South Africa he escaped the carping criticisms which had poured down on Phil Bennett in New Zealand. It was impossible not to like Billy as a person. I did not consider him to be a master tactician and, like Murphy, he paid too little attention to the backs, but he more than compensated for this by the example he set others both on and off the field. He had a marvellously even temperament. He was your genuine John Bull – brave, determined and a man of unimpeachable integrity.

In recent years there has been an increasing amount of talk about the abolition of Lions tours. The arguments are that they are time-consuming and that it is difficult if not well-nigh impossible to blend the characteristics of the four different countries into a winning combination. I could never agree with that view. There will always be tales of the Welsh huddling together in morose cliques; of half the Irish contingent being dipsomaniacs and the other half religious fanatics. But, generally speaking, Lions tours present unparalleled opportunities to forge friendships and to play the game at the highest possible level. It should be, and in 99 cases out of 100 it is, the height of a player's ambition to go on a Lions tour. I do not believe that individual countries would have more success than a composite side. How could Scotland, for example, possibly contemplate a victory in a Test series in New Zealand?

Some of the most enjoyable moments of my rugby career have been spent on Lions jaunts in the company both on and off the field of the likes of Gareth Edwards and Phil Bennett. I count it an honour and a privilege to have played with so many truly great players, and although the task has been far from easy, I have attempted to choose the side I believe to be the best, comprising the players with whom I have travelled on Lions tours.

For the purpose of this exercise let us imagine that my hamstrings and Achilles tendons have finally snapped, and that I am sitting with both legs in plaster on the touch line. So, with apologies to the many fine players I have been forced to leave out, here goes: J. P. R. Williams; John Carleton, Ian McGeechan, Dick Milliken and Mike Slemen; Phil Bennett and Gareth Edwards; Ian McLauchlan, Peter Wheeler and Fran Cotton; Bill Beaumont and Gordon Brown; Fergus Slattery, Tony Neary and Mervyn Davies. Syd Millar would be manager and coach.

13

The Spin-offs of a Rugby Life

To tour with the Lions is the ultimate goal of every British rugby player, and each of my three trips was a wonderful experience. But the rewards of playing the game at that level do not end there, and I have been very lucky at some of the marvellous spin-off perks which have come my way.

Two years after the British Lions tour to South Africa in 1980 I returned to Durban for a special charity goal-kicking competition which was organized by one of the churches out there to raise funds. Six of the best South African international goal-kickers were invited along with myself and Dusty Hare. We had to kick goals from a variety of positions in the field from the touch-line and from the middle of the field, beginning on the 25 and working our way back to the half-way line. We followed this up with half a dozen drop kicks from similar positions, and the leading four players advanced to the Grand Final. These proved to be the hot favourite, the legendary Springbok kicker Naas Botha, who shortly afterwards was signed by one of the big American football teams, Dusty Hare, myself and the surprise mystery guest. One of the famous Springboks was unable to attend at the last minute and they filled his spot with a little-known local club player.

We had managed to beat off the challenge of well-known Springbok experts like Ian McCallum and de Wet Ras, but in the final we were all unable to contain the local lad. He duly won the competition with Dusty and myself second equal and Naas Botha fourth. Full credit must go to the winner although I think it's fair to point out that it was not what would be called statistically significant because the sample of 20 kicks or so each was not a sufficient number to draw accurate conclusions. To make it more representative of our skill we would have needed to take nearer 200 kicks each, but there are much better ways of spending a week in Natal than thumping a rugby ball from dawn to dusk, as Dusty and I proved to our wives who had accompanied us on this unique trip.

Audrey and I were guests of Holiday Inn Hotels, and we had a fabulous week under the personal supervision of Rod Weinrich who organized some special excursions for us. We spent two days in a game park on a guided tour which was led by one of the wardens in his own landrover rather than in the usual tour bus. Looking back now from a safe distance it was an unforgettable outing but at the time it was hair-raising. He would stop the landrover every so often and tell us to walk into the bundu with him. We were petrified to join him and equally petrified to decline and thereby confess our trepidation. We walked amongst massive buffalo, wildebeest and giraffe and within 50 yards of rhino. The ranger explained we were downwind of them and perfectly safe because, basically, they are deaf and blind and rely almost exclusively on their sense of smell. I wondered what would happen if the wind changed direction, and he frightened the life out of Audrey by asking if she could run as fast as me. We concluded that the ranger and I might have made it to the sanctuary of the car but that there was a grave risk that Audrey might suffer a horn in a tender part of her anatomy. The other highlight of the safari was the meal late that evening. The ranger organized an open-air barbeque, known in South Africa as a braaivleis, in pitch darkness in the middle of the jungle. It was an eerie, exciting occasion because we could see nothing apart from the flames of the fire. And we could hear the snorts and grunts of animals all around us as well as the roar of lions in the distance. The ranger told us that that area was riddled with snakes and scorpions which caused me alarm and considerable discomfort because after a liberal gargle with the local beer I needed to relieve myself but was terrified of straying more than a yard from the ranger, and I could not face making the short journey to the nearest tree which meant I stood beside the fire, legs crossed, throughout the meal. A week beside an idyllic beach followed to cap a super holiday, and a couple of coaching sessions and an after-dinner speech were carried out all too willingly by me in return for the favours received. I was especially delighted that Audrey had had a great time after the years of hard work with the young children while I had been away training and playing and touring ever since we were married.

Audrey joined me on two other outstanding adventures on the other side of the world. In April 1978 the Zingari Richmond club in Dunedin invited myself, Jim Renwick and Ian McLauchlan, plus our wives, to New Zealand for the best part of three weeks to join in their centenary celebrations. We played one game in Dunedin, one in Wellington and one in Auckland, and they were all excellent games of rugby. It was a tremendous thrill for me to play in the same team as Bruce Robertson, Bill Osborne, Steve Pokere and Sid Going who proved to me then that he was just as great a player as Gareth Edwards. It was worth travelling the 13,000 miles just to play with these fabulous All Blacks, but we also had a great holiday under the personal supervision of Alan and Grace Mills, visiting the main tourist attractions and rounding off the trip with three days in the Bay of Islands in the very north. Alan and Grace explained that this sub-tropical holiday resort was regarded as paradise by every tourist and every New Zealander, and we fully agreed with these sentiments.

In May 1983, Audrey and I reached paradise once again when we set off to the Cayman Islands. These are situated between Cuba and Jamaica, and the captain of the rugby club, John Gibson, was originally from

Edinburgh. He was given the responsibility of finding a guest speaker, and when he kindly invited me, I can safely say it did not take long to make up my mind. We were feted for a wonderful week, and took full advantage of the glorious weather in the mid-eighties to indulge in the local water sports. I became quickly hooked on scuba diving although I think one of the main highlights for Audrey was discovering that we were on the same flight back to London from Miami as Prince Charles and Princess Diana.

During my career I met several members of the royal family from time to time when they turned up at internationals and were presented to the teams beforehand. That happened on a handful of occasions and it was always very special to shake hands and have a brief conversation with the Queen and Prince Philip. The icing on that particular cake came in December 1979 when I went, along with Audrey and my mother, to Buckingham Palace to receive the MBE. It was a rare treat to venture inside Buckingham Palace, and it was a day of high drama and excitement. We left our hotel in the West End in a panic because we were a shade late, and leapt into a taxi as quickly as we could. When we arrived at the Palace I realized we had left the tickets in the hotel. It took a great deal of explanation before we were eventually allowed to enter as I was not, apparently, the first person that day to arrive at the famous gates with the same story. I managed to convince the security men that my account of events was actually true. It was a doubly rewarding day for Scottish rugby because the BBC television commentator, Bill McLaren, was also there to receive the MBE. One of his pleasant little traits at international training sessions or on the afternoon of a big game as the players survey the pitch is to offer everyone his favourite mint sweets of which he seems to have a never-ending supply in his various pockets. I was two or three paces ahead of him in the queue and he leaned forward to slip me a mint a couple of minutes before it was my turn. The Queen asked me if

I was going to go on playing rugby for Scotland and I replied that I certainly hoped that I would. Bill went up a few moments later, and the Queen inquired what he specialized in. He explained he was a rugby commentator with the BBC, and Her Majesty immediately asked if, by any chance, he knew of a rugby player called Andy Irvine whom she had just met a few moments previously. He answered that he most certainly did, over a period of a dozen very happy years.

One interesting point the Queen may not have realized is that we actually had something in common. Both Her Majesty and myself shared an equine link with the royal race-horse trainer, Ian Balding. Whereas Her Majesty had a dozen top-class blue-blooded thoroughbreds each year in training with Ian, in 1975, in my own tiny, humble way, I joined the ranks of the race-horse owners when I took a 12th share in a two-year-old colt which we named the British Lion. The syndicate contained quite a few British Lions rugby players including Cliff Morgan, Gareth Edwards, Barry John, Fergus Slattery, Gordon Brown and myself, but my suspicions were first aroused in January that year when Gordon, Fergus and I visited the stables to chart the progress of our flying machine. In a three-furlong gallop with the horse, I finished a length ahead of Fergus with the horse six lengths away third, just a short head in front of G. L. Brown. The horse was apparently so fast on the gallops at Kingsclere that half the racing world expected him to produce a course record when he ran for the first time, and he started the odds-on favourite. But much to the disgust of those members of the syndicate who turned up to lead him into the winner's enclosure, he trailed in at the back of the field, having taken every possible precaution to avoid breaking sweat.

The next three races followed a similarly depressing pattern as he failed in the first three at 5 furlongs, 6 furlongs, and then 7 furlongs despite the totally unjustified blind faith of the British punting fraternity who poured on enough cash each time to ensure he started the odds-on favourite on every occasion. Ian Balding, former Cambridge University rugby blue and Bath and Somerset full back, is one of the top ten trainers in Britain, and having won such races as the Derby and the Prix de l'Arc de Triomphe with Mill Reef, knows almost all there is to know about racing. After the fourth successive humiliation in a row, he shrugged his shoulders and announced that the only problem with British Lion was his hatred of racing. The decision was taken never to run him again, but three months later the trainer had a brainwave. He replaced the formidable Joe Mercer, one of the strongest jockeys around, with a young, relatively weak, training apprentice called John Matthias. He was later to become a leading jockey but at that time was simply learning the tricks of the trade. Ian reckoned that if the horse thought he could do whatever he liked, he might just run somewhere near his true potential. The raw apprentice was given instructions to avoid kicking and whipping British Lion and to just allow him to run his own race. It was an ingenious tactical wheeze which worked to perfection and had only one minor drawback – the trainer did not confide in the syndicate! He felt we had all lost enough money already and wanted to spare us any further financial embarrassment. The handful of part-owners who did actually spot the horse was running in a selling race at Thirsk on Saturday 6 September took one of two sensible courses of action – they avoided going anywhere near a betting shop all day or they phoned their worst enemy to announce they had a gilt-edged certainty. The stalls opened, the horse settled in the middle of the 22 runners and gradually made up ground half way through the seven-furlong race. With two furlongs left he cruised up to challenge the leader, Thames, and at the furlong pole he drew clear of the field to win by an impressive two and a half lengths at the rewarding odds of 14–1. Not one of us had a penny on with the bookmakers and the first prize of £596 scarcely covered our gambling losses earlier in the season. What is worse, because we had won a selling race the horse was put up for auction immediately afterwards. A northern trainer, Harry Blackshaw, raised the bidding past what Ian Balding considered a sensible price and we lost the horse at the auction. My initial disillusionment with the world of horse racing has long since mellowed, and I'm pleased to report that Ian Balding has passed on the odd very good-priced winner in the past ten years so I will not hear a word said against him.

The one sure way I could have made a lot of money in the mid-seventies was not by backing race-horses but by turning rugby league. Only one club approached me prior to my first British Lions tour in 1974, but that was Salford who had two famous former rugby players in their team already, David Watkins and Keith Fielding, and they made persistent and regular overtures during the next few years. David phoned me several times between the end of 1973 and 1977 but the most direct approach came from Wigan. Shortly after I returned from South Africa in the autumn of 1974, I came home from the office one afternoon to find two men sitting in the lounge. They had been there for several hours, determined to see me, and once I arrived they wasted no time in making their offer. The spokesman was a grossly overweight fellow with a broad Lancashire accent. 'O.K. son, we are not here to beat about the bush and we're not here to waste our time or your time. We are here to offer you a straight £15,000 signing-on fee to turn professional for Wigan. The club have followed your career with Scotland and the British Lions, and we think you will do very well as a professional.

At the time I was earning £700 a year, and Audrey and I were about to become engaged. Suddenly a fat guy with a big cigar was offering me 20 times my annual salary to play rugby for a living. Audrey was visibly excited at the size of the offer and my mother, sitting in the opposite corner of the room, was nodding her head in full approval and was quick to offer maternal advice 'Take the money, son.' Without any hesitation, I told them I was not interested even if they offered me £100,000. I told them, tongue in cheek, I would want that sort of sum just to live in a place like Wigan let alone have to play rugby league as well. I am fiercely Scottish and I've always loved living in Edinburgh. I will never leave Scotland and certainly not to live in Wigan or Warrington or Workington. I might one day be tempted by Paris or Rome or Durban or Hong Kong but it is highly unlikely, however, the heart of industrial Lancashire holds no attraction. The Wigan heavies knew at once that they were wasting their time but they asked if I could think of any good Scottish full back who might be interested. I told them that the best young full back in the country was a guy from Kelso called George Fairbairn. To my amazement I read in the papers the following week that Fairbairn had signed for Wigan for a tiny fee. He was to progress rapidly and become one of the game's real stars and a regular member of the Great Britain rugby league team. It is an intriguing thought to reflect that if he had not gone to rugby league, he might have displaced me in the Scottish rugby union side.

The next good offer came from Widnes and it was to be far and away the biggest I ever received. They made contact with me after the 1977 British Lions tour to New Zealand, and they started talking to me in astronomical sums. They offered me the possibility of earning up to £75,000 in the first year with a large signing-on fee, appearance money, win bonuses and the prospect of further bonus money for playing in representative matches. They pointed out to me that if I survived five years in the game I would find playing rugby league a pretty lucrative existence. Although I was a young, married, family man at the time, earning pin money, I despatched the Widnes entourage just as summarily as I had done the Wigan and Salford representatives before and those from Hull, Leeds and St Helens afterwards. The Widnes spokesman was their current captain at the time, and he was hoping to become coach, but I convinced him in a couple of minutes that I loved rugby union and playing for Scotland and Heriot's far too much to ever contemplate switching codes.

The other offers I received were made by middle-men on behalf of clubs with the exception of Workington who made direct approaches in the late seventies. One of the initial contacts from Salford was a guy called Tom Mitchell with whom I became quite friendly over the years. Eventually, he became chairman of Workington, and they expressed an interest each year from 1978 to 1981 but it was on a friendly and informal basis and they were well aware that deep down I had no real intention of ever deserting rugby union.

The only money I did earn as an amateur rugby union player was when I competed in the 'Superstars' television programmes, and my prize money was then always paid directly by the organizers to the Scottish Rugby Union. I told the SRU the names of the charities that I wanted to share the money and the Secretary of the Union then dispersed the largesse according to my wishes.

1978 was the first year I took part in 'Superstars' at Cwmbran in Wales, and I genuinely believe I could have won if I had trained specifically for it. I would much rather that we had all turned up for the weekend without any idea which events were in store for us. That would have been the fairest way to discover the best all-round sportsman. As it was, I sat in a canoe for the first time ever at the event itself whereas Brian Jacks, the judo star, had been training hard for months just to win 'Superstars' and earn considerable prize money. Jacks and the water skier, Mike Hazelwood, had spent three or four months perfecting every one of the events in which we took part and that gave them a huge advantage. As an amateur sportsman with a very demanding job and a young family to support there was no remote possibility that I could do any special training at all for the more unusual events. I fared badly in the cycling because I honestly do not think I had sat on a bicycle once in the previous ten years, and had I done a little better at either the cycling or the canoe race then I would have won instead of being a close third behind Jacks and Hazelwood.

My placing in that first event was good enough to get me to the finals three months later and once more I finished third of the eight competitors behind Brian Jacks, yet again, and the former long jump Olympic champion, Lyn Davies. Finishing third in the British final turned out to be sufficiently good for me to get an invitation to compete in the World Final of 'Superstars' in March 1979 in America. Unfortunately, it clashed with a vital league match for my club Heriot's against West of Scotland, and there was no way I would have missed that game for an enjoyable, but meaningless, event like 'Superstars'.

I was invited again in 1982 to the British event in Nottingham. I finished second overall behind the athlete Stuart Matthews but I had some satisfaction in beating Mike Hazelwood who reckoned he was pretty fit but had not had any time for regular, steady training for the specialized events like archery, pistol shooting, football, cycling and canoeing. That was a most enjoyable weekend mixing with the other competitors like Mike Channon the England footballer, Tony Knowles the snooker player, and Kevin Jolley from badminton. I was invited to the major finals later that year in Europe but I was unable to take time off work and that was the last time I competed individually in 'Superstars'.

I did have one fantastic weekend, however, competing for rugby union in a similar event called 'Superteams'. On the Thursday night in Bath, the rugby guys – Jeff Squire and Graham Price from Wales, Nick Jeavons, Marcus Rose and John Carleton from England, and Jim Renwick and myself from Scotland – had a great night sitting in the bar until the early hours of the morning reliving all the good times we had shared together and consuming a reasonable amount of beer. We were pitched against the Wheelies the next day – cyclists, motor cyclists and motor racing drivers – and they had all gone to bed early, taking it very seriously. Suffice to say, we won convincingly.

The nice thing about the 'Superstars' weekends was that they ran a couple of different programmes concurrently. That meant they might have a senior or veterans 'Superstars' at the same time as our event. I remember having a super evening meeting and chatting to Bobby Charlton, Brian Close, Billy Walker and Stirling Moss, and if it had not been for rugby initially and subsequently 'Superstars' I would never have met such fascinating sportsmen. Nor would I have met face to face two of my favourite sporting heroes – Jack Nicklaus and Gary Player.

Golf is my second sporting love and is now rapidly taking over from rugby, and I was delighted to be invited to a special charity event during the Glasgow Chamber Bi-centennial celebrations. Jack Nicklaus was the star attraction at the Whitecraigs course in Glasgow, and the successful formula was for three amateurs to challenge him over two holes each. This meant that over the 18 holes, 27 different amateur players – mostly well-known sporting personalities – had a cut at beating the Golden Bear over two holes. All three amateurs drove off along with Nicklaus and then, once we'd reached the green, one amateur nearest the hole would putt out against Jack Nicklaus. At the first of my two holes, I missed the green altogether with my second so I was bombed out. But at the second hole, I hit my iron shot to within five feet of the pin. As Jack Nicklaus addressed his second shot, I pointed out to him that he had that eight iron to win the hole. He clipped the ball to about eight feet from the flag and then proceeded to miss the putt. I sunk my five-footer to win the hole to allow me to relate *ad nauseam* over dinner the story of how, the last time I played Jack Nicklaus at golf, I beat him!

I must say he was tremendous fun and good company, and I was agreeably surprised how relaxed, easy going and sociable he was. It was also a thrill and a half to play with him and admire at close range the sheer perfection of his golf. I dare say he is a hard-headed businessman when push comes to shove, and doubtless he is a very tough competitor on the golf circuit, but that day he was a perfect gentleman and he made a lasting impression on everyone who was lucky enough to cross his path.

In South Africa in 1980 during the Lions tour a few of us were fortunate to cross the path of Gary Player. He invited Johnny Robbie, Clive Woodward, Peter Wheeler and myself to his ranch near Johannesburg. He showed us the sort of training he did every day to keep fit, and it was so demanding that I reckon he would have sorted out Brian Jacks and the rest in 'Superstars'. He is much smaller and lighter than Nicklaus, and the weight training and exercising he does to compensate for his lack of sheer ballast is quite phenomenal. He showed us a special solid lead golf club, a driver, which was incredibly heavy and which he uses to practise his swing every day. He held it outstretched with just 2 fingers and asked us to try to do the same. Even a pocket Tarzan like Peter Wheeler failed hopelessly. Gary Player has forearms like Popeye which explains how he can hit the ball so far. I marvelled at his totally dedicated attitude to his sport. He is a fitness fanatic and sticks rigidly to a special diet.

He is a philosopher who relishes the pressure and tension of professional golf, but off the course he was able to relax and entertain us royally all afternoon. He seemed to know as much about race-horses and rugby as he did about golf, but after my racing experiences I managed to steer the conversation back to golf the moment anyone went off at a tangent. Nevertheless, thanks to a decade playing rugby at international level I have had a lot of fun and broadened my horizons enormously, and from so many exciting peripheral activities I would select the time spent with Jack Nicklaus and Gary Player as extra special highlights which I will always recall with particular pleasure.

14

Rugby Today – and Tomorrow?

The game of rugby has come a long way since I first played for Scotland in 1972 but I think it has mostly developed in the right direction and I have very few grievances or complaints to raise as I reflect on the various vicissitudes of life with Heriot's and Scotland. I would never have believed 15 years ago that Scotland would have voted in favour of a Rugby Union World Cup but I am delighted that they have done so because I think it is such an exciting project. It will give the opportunity to the emerging rugby nations of the world such as the exciting Japanese, Koreans and Fijians, to rub shoulders with the established heavyweights of the International Board countries. Unfortunately, the World Cup has arrived a few years too late for me as I would have loved to have participated in such a novel tournament. I'm sure it will encourage and foster 15-a-side rugby among the smaller nations of the rugby-playing fraternity in exactly the same way as the Cathay Pacific Sevens have helped in Hong Kong each year with their tournament.

It is often so much easier to knock the establishment than offer praise and support, but I reckon the SRU has done a better job than they have generally been given credit for, and in many ways have led the four home unions with their image of a better future.

They have totally restructured the game, and have a better club system than any other country in the world.

They have the ideal district championship which now encompasses the Anglo-Scots as well, and that means the selectors are able to watch the best 75 players who are eligible to play for Scotland battling it out in ten important matches each season before the international campaign commences. From watching those players perform under pressure they can select the best international team. Few people get picked for Scotland from outside the First Division of the club championship, and virtually no-one is selected if they fail to make one of the district sides, but this is the right philosophy because it is essential for the cream to rise to the top and then to pick from strength. If Kenny Dalglish had to play for Wrexham every week, a team languishing at the wrong end of the English Fourth Division, instead of for Liverpool, his general sharpness and standard would inevitably suffer. He would be surrounded by poorer footballers and would be playing against poorer players, and that is bound to have a detrimental effect. That is the root cause of the trouble with English rugby, so we should be grateful to the SRU for organizing the excellent structure in Scotland. In particular, the introduction of league rugby in Scotland has generated much more interest in the game. There is far greater media coverage of club matches which has led to larger crowds in direct contrast to the diminishing volume of spectators at soccer games. Club training is now much better organized with players turning out much more frequently at training.

This is not to say that everything has always been perfect because that is not the case, but the SRU have made changes for the better and there are far fewer grounds for discontent now than at any time in my experience. Long gone are the days which I well remember when we got one navy blue international jersey for the first match of the season and that was it. If we swapped after the game we had to buy a new one from the union for the next international. In my first two seasons, I always swapped my jersey and ended up with a bill for eight of them, which came to a tidy sum in those days for a young student trying to make ends meet. Nowadays Scotland, like all the other unions, give their players a new jersey for each international.

Similarly, there is a much more enlightened attitude to the wives and girlfriends of the players now than there was in the dark old days. In the early Seventies they were ignored to the extent that no-one acknowledged their existence but now the ladies are invited to a special dinner of their own on the Saturday evening, to the party afterwards and their hotel accommodation is paid by the union. After all, the players make a significant contribution to filling Murrayfield for two or three internationals every year which bring in gate money of over a quarter of a million pounds per match and it was quite wrong in the past to scrimp when it came to looking after the players.

It was always the little things which annoyed and upset people. I remember in Bill Beaumont's last game for England I kicked a penalty from inside my own half right at the end to draw the match and, in a moment of totally reckless elation later that night, without giving serious thought to the grave financial implications of my wanton and frivolous act, I ordered a pot of coffee and a round of sandwiches in my hotel room for myself, Jim Renwick and our wives. The bill came to a staggering £7.80 and I had the temerity to sign for it on the room bill. The SRU wasted no time in chasing me the following week for the money which, in the end, I had to repay. In fairness, it was really just a minor niggle but my argument was that the four of us could have been at the after match party drinking buckets and buckets of champagne, whisky, beer or whatever absolutely free until we drowned in the stuff, but a cup of coffee had to be paid for by the players themselves. Such rigidity and inflexibility is fast disappearing and the great thing now is that the old demarcation zone of 'them and us' has now vanished and there is a good rapport between the players and the SRU committee men.

It is easy to criticize any committee but before critics

start shouting from the rooftops I suggest they spend a year on a rugby club committee and appreciate the massive sacrifices each person has to make in time and energy to ensure the smooth running of a club. I spent several years on the Heriot's committee and as a result I have only the highest respect and admiration for anyone prepared to devote his life to the well-being of others. That applies to Heriot's, to Edinburgh district and, indeed, to the SRU. There is a great deal of hard work required of anyone who joins the union and, if very occasionally, someone does it as part of an ego trip for self-aggrandizement, the huge majority are there for the good of the game. They sit on all sorts of different committees trying their very best to safeguard the interests of every one of the thousands of rugby players and hundreds of clubs in Scotland.

In appreciating the SRU for their administrative and organizational abilities and their total commitment of rugby, it does not mean that they have never made bad mistakes. I felt their treatment of Gordon Brown was a mistake although I can accept they acted in all good faith. Gordon did retaliate very vigorously to a disgraceful incident off the ball perpetrated by one Allan Hardie at Murrayfield in a match which was televised. The shameful incident and Brown's instinctive and natural reaction were captured on celluloid for all to see. I have always abhorred violent play, and would be delighted if the roughnecks were hounded out of the game. No club, let alone international side, should ever pick dirty players, and it is to the shame of rugby that a number of such rogues still seem to survive. It is interesting to see which countries in Europe pick players who have a bad track record and reputation for being sent off. I think Scotland and Ireland would be some way below Wales and France in this respect and that does not reflect creditably on these latter two countries. In my own view, the instigator of the trouble during that inter-district game in 1976 Allan Hardie, was let off with a sentence of 18 months suspension for the unprovoked mayhem which he had caused in trampling all over Gordon Brown who was trapped on the ground. Brown received an unnecessarily stiff suspension of three months for his retaliation. He was effectively banned for the whole of the 1977 season because the sentence was announced in December 1976 and, in fact, he was never to play for Scotland again. In this instance, the SRU over-reacted. Gordon was one of the best half-dozen lock forwards in world rugby in the seventies and his loss to Scottish international rugby was immeasurable. He could have given three or four more valuable years of service to Scotland, but his heart and soul were never in it after that tragic incident and it is no coincidence that the famine at international level which was experienced north of the border began in 1977. The SRU in boldly trying to eliminate dirty play, led the way with stiff sentences but, sadly, no other country followed suit.

The other psychological blow which affected the morale of the team at the same time was the decision to discontinue the à la carte menu at our team hotel during the weekend of an international. At the Thursday and Friday meals, a set menu appeared instead because it was much less expensive. This was an infuriatingly trivial act of penny-pinching which did precious little to build up the confidence of the players; they were told by the coach how wonderful and indispensable they were and then at the same time they were treated as second-class citizens by the executive committee. Happily that has all changed again as the SRU lead the way towards the twenty-first century.

On the playing side two grey areas have surfaced. Players in the international squad are becoming increasingly fed up with the length and regularity of training sessions and this problem is not peculiar to Scotland. I think players everywhere in the northern hemisphere are finding too many demands being made on their time and they become exasperated when so little benefit accrues at the end of a long, tiring training session. Often such squad get-togethers are dragged out for three or four hours and players depart jaded and bored rather than invigorated and inspired. If this trend continues then the result will be that players will retire much earlier. The other area of controversy is peculiar to Scotland. The clubs still stubbornly refuse to sanction the use of replacements in league matches and, as I explained earlier in the book, I think this is absolutely wrong. I sincerely hope common sense will prevail on this issue in the very near future.

Also I feel strongly that there should be some fundamental changes in the laws of the game. I believe that rugby at the highest level is now a duller game than it was ten years ago and I think it is important to have laws which ensure that the most attractive style of play is, more often than not, the most successful one. I would advocate altering the scoring system for a start. I would award five points for the try and would scrap the conversion altogether. If it was decided to keep the try at four points then I would suggest that all conversions irrespective of where the try was scored should be taken from a spot 25 yards out bang in front of the posts. If it was still worth two points for a conversion that would make a goal worth six points, but my preference is firmly for the five-point try and no conversions.

The whole purpose of rugby should be to spend 80 minutes scoring as many tries as possible and it is important to produce a scoring system commensurate with such a philosophy. To further enhance the value of scoring tries I would scrap the drop goal altogether and reduce the penalty goal to just two points. Under my scoring system the guarantee of five points for a try as against two points for a penalty, might well persuade backs to run the ball more. For all acts of foul play, I would recommend that the penalty, worth two points, irrespective of where the offence took place, be taken on the centre spot of the 25 directly in front of the posts. I would also like to see an increase in the use of the differential penalty. Apart from acts of foul play, dangerous play or persistent infringement, I do not think penalty kicks at goal should ever be allowed. I have always thought it wrong that a side who never manage to trespass inside the opposition half throughout the whole of a match, and, in consequence, never vaguely threaten to score a try, can actually win by landing two penalties from the half-way line. I would endorse a proposition to considerably extend the use of the differential penalty.

It is my contention that the better side would win far more regularly than it does now if these suggestions became law. No longer would a team win against the run of play by scoring six penalties to four tries. At the moment there is far too much emphasis placed on the necessity to include a good goal-kicker in a team. Although I have kicked thousands of points during the past 20 years, I really feel very strongly that penalty goals are ruining the game as a spectacle. Goal-kicking has had an absurdly disproportionate effect on the results of important matches for as long as I can remember and I would completely eradicate the possi-bility of such injustices happening in the future. In recent years the game has become more like a game of chess with the stalemate situation predominant far too often. The prevalent strategy in important matches is to have the half backs boot the ball into the opposition half of the field before contemplating an attacking ploy. I have played in far too many games over the years where the coach, and, dare I say, the forwards, have made it abundantly clear that anything which smacks of positive thinking in one's own half is not to be encouraged – in fact, quite the reverse. Such a basic philosophy is very sad for the game and its future. It is quite alien to my view on how the game should be played, although I do concede that the chances of winning, or rather not losing, are greatly increased by such a negative approach. The best solution to counter attack such stagnant play would be to change the laws.

As I have emphasized many times already, the influence of the weather should never be underestimated. It is very difficult to play good rugby in appalling conditions and it would make a great deal more sense to begin the Five Nations Championship a full month and preferably six weeks later. Instead of starting in the middle of January, I suggest the championship should commence on the first Saturday in March and go through to the end of April. Even the current modest standard of the championship would improve if the internationals were played in the spring rather than in the depths of winter.

One other major influence on the course of an international is the attitude and ability of the referee. There have been too many moderate referees of late and we have to question a system which puts three referees forward from each country and ensures that sooner or later they will all be given international matches. The selectors do not pick the third-best scrum half for a crunch international just because they feel it is his turn and yet that is precisely what happens when it comes to appointing the referee. My own ideal referee is someone who is absolutely firm and stands no nonsense, whilst also having a genuine feeling for the game. He should enter into the spirit and, strictly within the laws, he should encourage open rugby. It is important to make full use of the advantage law. It is conceivable that no one referee can encompass everything but a blend of my favourite two, Norman Sanson and Georges Domercq, would go a long way along the road to perfection.

The media tend to be critical of referees and I feel some sympathy for the man in the middle now because when an incident is shown on television in slow motion for the umpteenth time they can be seen to be horribly at fault. Their life is made even harder by the fact that half the players, especially the forwards, do everything in their power to outwit the hapless referee by hook or by crook.

I have been fortunate throughout my career that the Scottish press have been pretty good to me and generally when they have been critical, it has not been without reason. Writers like Brian Meek and Peter Donald in the

Express and *Mail*, Hugh Young in the *Daily Record*, Bill
Lothian and Reg Prophit in the *Edinburgh Evening News*,
Bill McLaren and Bill McMurtrie in the *Glasgow Herald*
and Norman Mair in the *Scotsman*, have all supported
Scottish rugby 100 per cent through the good times and
the bad. I am sure the role of a rugby correspondent is
not easy because when things go wrong, as they invariably did in the late seventies, the public want blood, but
to their credit the Scottish writers have usually shown a
basic sympathy and loyalty which the players have
respected. Unlike some of the English, Welsh or Australian press, when the going gets tough the Scottish media
have supported the players and the game.

Happily, the Scottish press and the players usually
mix well and one of the great bonuses of winning the
Grand Slam in 1984 was the fact that all these lads were
at last able to write the sort of stories they had always
dreamed of writing. I have always felt that Norman Mair
and Bill McLaren are two of the great rugby authorities
in international terms, but the bulk of the rest of the
Scottish press have also been very fair and have shown a
commendable sense of decency during the past 15 years.
I like to think that the press of Scotland are much closer
to the players than they are in other countries. They
become part of the whole set-up, part of the travelling
circus and they share with us the moments of elation and
dejection and they are better able to sense and thus
report the mood and the atmosphere before, during and
after a major international.

The press can be very influential. When the subject of
a World Cup was first proposed, it was greeted with
approval by the media. The more they wrote approving-
ly, the more the idea was fostered. Eventually, in March
1985, it was put to the vote at the International Board
Conference and it was carried by the narrowest possible
margin. The SRU according to the prevailing rumour
were not sold on the idea hook, line and sinker, but – and
this shows how much they have progressed in the last
decade – they consulted with a select group of the senior

players and when they discovered that these players were almost unanimously in favour of a World Cup, they determined to vote in support of the proposal. I think it is the most exciting of concepts and I am certain that when it takes place in Australia and New Zealand in 1987 it will be a fantastic boost for the game worldwide.

People have said that a World Cup, generating perhaps £20 million in gate receipts, worldwide television rights and advertising, might be the first slippery steps towards a headlong slide in the direction of a professional game. I am sure that this is total poppycock. The tournament will be all over in less than a month. The teams will arrive, play four or five matches, watch the semi-finals and finals and then return home. At no stage can money possibly pass hands and there is no rugby player in the world who would need any financial incentive before agreeing to take part in the first ever World Cup. Such hallucinations are conceived in the fertile minds of neurotic day-dreamers. Let me reassure such fantasizers, such Walter Mitty clones, that people like myself have played and always will play rugby for fun and enjoyment and that the game will always remain amateur. It is a rough, tough, physical game which brings together people of every race, creed and colour from every possible socio-economic background and with this totally cosmopolitan backcloth it is surely the greatest team game in the world. Rugby has survived for over a hundred years as an amateur sport and I fervently hope and believe it will survive the next hundred as well.

It is a character builder and it naturally demands an interwoven fellowship and comradeship lacking elsewhere. There is no place for the selfish individual and each star is totally dependent on the 14 satellites who surround him. Rugby is the proof that the chain is as strong as its weakest link and that gritty aspect is part of the undeniable glamour of the sport. It would be tragic if rugby ever changed; I do not believe it will. It is the last of the great amateur sports and I hope it will draw strength from this and consolidate its present position. It is a game I would heartily recommend to any aspiring youngster.

I can look back now on a hundred highlights a year which will comfort me in my dotage. In the final analysis, though I loved my tours with the British Lions and I suppose it is nice to have played in more Lions Tests than any other Scotsman, my happiest memories will be of playing for Heriot's and Scotland. Very little in life has given me a greater thrill and more pleasure than helping Heriot's pull off an unexpected league win at Goldenacre and playing a part in winning the championship probably meant more to me than anything else I ever achieved.

Thanks to rugby I have a golden treasure chest of memorabilia I can sift through in the future when I wonder what I did with my youth. I'll remember swinging a golf club with Jack Nicklaus and Gary Player with particular affection and nostalgia, and I will remember many of the other peripheral activities which have come my way as a happy by-product of playing rugby. These were all very nice and enjoyable, but much more important to me was the feeling sitting in the dressing room at Lancaster Park in Christchurch on 9 July 1977, when I had been in a winning team against New Zealand for the first and only time in my life. Much more important to me was the feeling in the pit of my stomach as my last-minute penalty gave us a dramatic victory against England in 1974, after I had almost cost Scotland the match earlier. Much more important to me than bare statistics was the huge fun I have had playing rugby in 21 different countries. Much more important to me was the honour of being the first British player to turn out for the French Barbarians and nothing can beat the crack of joining my team mates at training on Tuesdays and Thursdays at Goldenacre. I have loved every minute of it and I have met, played with and played against all the great players and the great characters in the game. In February 1985 a few Scottish and Irish internationals were invited to France during

207

the weekend of the Scotland–France match to play in an invitation golf tournament. The remarkable Moss Keane, having hacked the golf course to shreds, drastically decimating the Parisian worm population, proceeded to imbibe as only Mossie, in full flow, could. Typically, he went to bed so late on the Saturday morning after the Friday night out on the town that he was still sound asleep in the hotel when the match at Parc des Princes ended. *Plus ça change.*

The people, the games and the incidents are what really mattered. Rugby is a great leveller and ensures that there is no place for the smug, self-centred individual. I have known exactly what it is like to feel like a king at Murrayfield in a moment of triumph and also what it is like to feel like a leper in a moment of despair. I am just grateful that I have had more good times than bad and that the sport has been so incredibly kind to me. I can never disguise the fact that I simply love playing rugby. At the very end of my playing days in 1985 I made a return after an injury in Heriot's seconds against Gala YM in a match which Heriot's normally lost by a wide margin. That day we played our hearts out although we still lost narrowly. Such a close defeat was a moral victory and throwing the ball around in cavalier style we gave the natives the shock of their lives. It was a tremendously satisfying performance. I relished the challenge and was proud to be a member of the Heriot's 2nd XV that day because we exceeded all expectations. Nobody can ask for more and I am grateful for all the wonderful opportunities I've had from playing rugby. For a long time I wondered if there was life after playing for Heriot's and Scotland. I know now that there is. And just as I have enjoyed the last 15 years as a player, for the next 15 years people down Goldenacre and Murrayfield way had better get used to a passionate old-timer screaming encouragement and shouting for the two teams which have been such an integral part of a wonderful life.

Career Record

Year	Opponent	Results	Tries	Conversions	Penalties
1972	New Zealand	Lost 14–9			2
1973	France	Lost 16–13			
	Wales	Won 10–9			
	Ireland	Won 19–14			
	England	Lost 20–13		1	
	President's XV	Won 27–16		2	1
1974	Wales	Lost 6–0			
	England	Won 16–14	1	1	2
	Ireland	Lost 9–6			2
	France	Won 19–6		1	2
	Ireland	Won 20–13			2
	France	Lost 10–9			3
	Wales	Won 12–10			
	England	Lost 7–6			
	New Zealand	Lost 24–0			
	Australia	Won 10–3			
1975	France	Lost 13–6			
	Wales	Lost 28–6	1		
1976	England	Won 22–12		2	2

209

Year	Opponent	Results	Tries	Conversions	Penalties
1977	Ireland	Won 15–6			4
	England	Lost 26–6			2
	Ireland	Won 21–18			2
	France	Lost 23–3			1
1978	Wales	Lost 18–9	1	1	
	Ireland	Lost 12–9	1		
	France	Lost 19–16			
	England	Lost 15–0			
	New Zealand	Lost 18–9		1	
1979	Wales	Lost 19–13	1	1	3
	England	Draw 7–7			1
	Ireland	Draw 11–11	1		1
	France	Lost 21–17	1	1	1
	New Zealand	Lost 20–6	1		2
1980	Ireland	Lost 22–15		2	1
	France	Won 22–14	2	1	2
	Wales	Lost 17–6		1	
	England	Lost 30–18		2	2
1981	France	Lost 16–9			1
	Wales	Won 15–6	1*	1	
	England	Lost 23–17			1

	Results	Tries	Conversions	Penalties
Ireland	Won 10–9			1
New Zealand	Lost 11–4			2
New Zealand	Lost 40–15		1	4
Romania	Won 12–6			5
Australia	Won 24–15		1	2
1982 England	Draw 9–9		1	
Ireland	Lost 21–12			3
France	Won 16–7		1	
Wales	Won 34–18		4	
Australia	Won 12–7		1	1
Australia	Lost 33–9			3
		10	25	61
		(40 points)	(50 points)	(183 points)

TOTAL: 273 points

* penalty try

	Results	Tries	Conversions	Penalties
British Lions Tests				
1974 3rd Test v. South Africa	Won 26–9		1	2
4th Test v. South Africa	Draw 13–13	1		1

Year	Match	Results	Tries	Conversions	Penalties
1977	1st Test v. New Zealand	Lost 16–12			1
	2nd Test v. New Zealand	Won 13–9			1
	3rd Test v. New Zealand	Lost 19–7			
	4th Test v. New Zealand	Lost 10–9			1
1980	2nd Test v. South Africa	Lost 26–19			
	3rd Test v. South Africa	Lost 12–10	1		
	4th Test v. South Africa	Won 17–13	2	1	6
TOTAL: 28 points			(8 points)	(2 points)	(18 points)
GRAND TOTAL: 301 points			12 (48 points)	26 (52 points)	67 (201 points)

212